Praise for Clash of th...

"*Clash of the Couples* is hilarious and relatable, full of absurd arguments that will leave you shaking your head while feeling better about your own squabbles. Forget spats over money and parenting, these gems include college boobs, food poisoning during a hurricane, and the important question, 'Would you still think I was hot if I lost all my limbs?' Highly recommend!"

~ *Kristi Campbell, Finding Ninee*

"One minute it's so hilarious you're reading excerpts out loud to your spouse, the next it's so embarrassingly accurate that you're hiding it from them."

~ *Vicki Lesage, author of Confessions of a Paris Party Girl*

"This collection of frank and funny stories about surviving marriage should be required reading for all newlyweds. Every battle, detailed in Technicolor brilliance, may not have a clear winner but as a reader you sure feel victorious."

~ *Brooke Takhar, missteenussr.com*

"The stories in *Clash of the Couples* take readers on a realistic peek into lovers' arguments that range from travel planning to QVC apples. Regardless of the topic or the dialogue, most couples can identify with the eruptive emotions. We relate to the absurdity of the quarrels and sigh with relief that humor saves the relationships."

~ *Julaina Kleist, Time to Write Now*

"*Clash of the Couples* truly puts love in a chokehold! Get ready to laugh, cry, relate, and possibly find something new to argue about! A relationship just isn't branded until you've stamped it with a clash!"

~ *Tandra Wilkerson, Thriller Mom*

"*Clash of the Couples* brings to light the truth about things we don't always want to admit happen. I was constantly laughing and/or agreeing because it was as if I was reading about my own relationship."

~ *Alyssa, Babies, Bloodhounds, and Booze*

"These writers are keeping it real, sharing the dirt on some of their less idyllic relationship moments. Think you're alone in your ludicrous arguments with your spouse? From vacation fails to controversial TV tables, every reader who has ever been part of a couple is sure to find something here that hits close to home."

~ *Deborah Coombs, RaisingMyBoys.net*

CLASH

OF THE

Couples

A HUMOROUS COLLECTION OF COMPLETELY ABSURD
Lovers' Squabbles AND RELATIONSHIP SPATS

BLUE LOBSTER BOOK CO.

BLUE LOBSTER BOOK CO.

Clash of the Couples:
A Humorous Collection of Completely Absurd Lovers' Squabbles
and Relationship Spats

Written By Some VERY Brave Men and Women

Published in the United States by Blue Lobster Book Co.
ISBN: 978-0-9899553-3-1

Visit us online:
www.bluelobsterbookco.com

Edited by Gayle Roberts
(gayle_d_roberts@yahoo.com)

Cover and book design by Ashton Designs
(www.ashtondesigns.co.uk)

This book is dedicated to the couples who make it work—day in and day out—even when they clash and, most importantly, our partners and spouses without whom this project would not have been possible.

Contents

Acknowledgments

This book would not have come to life without the support of our family, friends, and fellow writers. You have our undying love and gratitude. Thanks for believing in us!

We'd also like to thank the following bloggers for taking part in our cover reveal (you totally rock!):

Tamara Bowman of Tamara (Like) Camera

SauvBlancMom of Mommy Needs Wine, Not Whine

Mama Rabia of The Lieber Family Blog

NJ Rongner of A Cookie Before Dinner

Celeste Snodgrass, Kim Schenkelberg, and Natalie Guenther of It's Really 10 Months

Kristen Daukas of Four Hens and a Rooster

Traci O'Neill of A Day in the Life of a Drama Queen's Momma

Jennifer Iacovelli of Another Jennifer Blog + Writing Lab

Tracy Sano of Tracy on the Rocks

C. Lee Reed of Helicopter Mom and Just Plane Dad

Carrie Groves of Ponies and Martinis

Toby Shoemaker of Dumbass News

Last, but certainly not least, we HAVE to give a shout out to the original couple who provided us with so much inspiration—*Adam and Eve*. No duo has ever rocked leaf-adorned pasties better than you.

Introduction

It happened on a Friday night—a smash-up of separate, but interconnected events that led to what I now refer to as The Applebee's Love Tsunami.

Somehow my husband and I had managed to escape the confines of parenthood to enjoy a night out alone. As we scarfed down mozzarella sticks and a handful of other calorie-happy appetizers, I overheard a woman say, "You never listen to me." And it didn't end there. In a matter of thirty seconds, she had rattled off about twenty different loaded statements and questions not really meant for response:

You have no idea what I like and what I don't like, do you?

I never eat seafood. Why would you order shrimp as an appetizer?

I don't care if there's cocktail sauce. It's gross. I'm not eating that crap.

I should've waited until after we had ordered to use the bathroom. I would have ordered something good.

No, I don't want to call the waitress over and order something else. You know I don't eat seafood.

We've been together for twelve years. TWELVE YEARS, JIM! You should know by now that I don't eat anything that comes out of the ocean!

Do you even know what color eyes I have? Here, look closely. THEY'RE BROWN! Unlike the Baltic Sea.

Jim was in some serious trouble.

As cunningly as a preying housecat, I pretended to check out the hockey game on TV while peeking behind me to catch a glimpse of Shrimp Hater and poor ole' Jim. They were seated on opposite sides of a sprawling table. Shrimp Hater was still pounding Jim in a full-on verbal assault. Jim sat relatively immobile, staring vacantly at the woman who was most likely his wife.

Their waitress showed up with a mounded platter full of pink delicacies. Before the food made its way onto the table, Jim raised his left hand as if to say, "Stop." He then said, "My wife is allergic to shrimp. Can we order something else?"

Oh, Jim, you poor, poor soul. Even I now know that she's not allergic.

Before he could say another word, his wife stood up, pushed by their server, and stormed from the restaurant. Jim quickly trailed behind, looking like he had been kicked directly in the love torpedoes.

When I turned back around to enlighten my husband, the "bom bom bom bom" melody of his favorite mobile game echoed throughout our side of the restaurant.

"Are you really playing *Clash of Clans* on our one night out in almost two years?"

"My village just got raided."

"Your village just got raided? You know what's not getting raided tonight? Can you figure that one out?"

As I sat watching Shrimp Hater and poor ole' Jim arguing in the parking lot, an energy-efficient light bulb went off in my head. Couples fight over some *really* stupid shit. And that's where the idea for this book was born. While my husband saved some washing wenches from an opposing army of heathens, I secretly began planning *Clash of the Couples.*

Although I'm not an expert on relationships, I've been in my fair share of couples' conundrums. I've also witnessed—time and time again—the finger pointing, word jabbing, and eye rolling that often accompanies the relationship spat. Shrimp Hater and poor ole' Jim, my husband and me, Brangelina, possibly even Adam and Eve—we've all had our ridiculously heated moments in the name of love.

As we left the restaurant, I noticed the formerly bickering couple making out like teenagers in the front seat of a car. I turned to my own husband and gave him a smooch. So he killed some goblins and pillaged a village during our one night out in nearly 730 days. So what? There are worse things in life.

Don't sweat the small stuff, and never go to bed angry at the one you love.

Enjoy the book!

Crystal Ponti

You Want Some College Boobs?

By Crystal Ponti

THERE'S A FIFTEEN-YEAR AGE DIFFERENCE BETWEEN MY husband and me. I'm the old one. He's the spring chicken. Most days this isn't an issue. Other days—"college boobs" comes up in the browsing history of our computer. Despite the years that separate us, I'm not typically insecure. My body has grown and birthed five kids. I'm the walking equivalent of a 1984 Honda Civic—that's still on the road. I have dings, dents, and depressions, in all the wrong places. Thankfully, my husband loves me, battle wounds and all.

So I'm not sure why college boobs singed my nose hairs and sent me on a buffalodic stampede. All guys look at boobs on the Internet, *right*? Would I have been more at ease if the search had read "sagging tits with stretch marks"?

Shocked and PMS-driven, I frantically clicked on each of the links that appeared after college boobs. There was nothing hardcore. Not like what I had expected. There were a few YouTube videos of wet T-shirt contests. Several pages of wild sorority parties. And some straggling Google images of nothing more than twenty-somethings sporting bikinis. It was a nippleless search extravaganza.

But I was pissed. Peeved off.

I paced back and forth, leaving a scuff trail across the hardwood floors. I paced until he arrived home from work later that night.

He was barely through the door before I nailed him. "College boobs, huh? You want some of those?"

His happy, "Honey, I'm home!" look quickly turned to, "Shit, I'm dead!"

"Well? Do you want young tits? Or did Larry the Porn Star get his hands on our computer?"

I expected plausible denial. Or sarcastic wit. Instead, all he could mutter was, "Books."

Books? What was he talking about? I clearly said BOOBS.

"Books? Are you listening to me? I said 'boobs.' You were looking up college boobs!"

"No. I wasn't actually looking up college boobs. I needed to order a book for one of my classes. I typed in college boobs accidentally and—"

"And what?" I interrupted.

"*Got carried away?*" It was more a question than a statement.

"And I'm supposed to believe that?"

"Here. Let me turn on the computer and show you. You'll see that earlier in the day I was searching for college books."

"Forget it. You don't need to justify your actions or prove anything to me."

"But I want to."

As the computer whirred to life, I felt like a big jerk standing over his shoulder. Was I really so caught up on young boobies that my husband felt the need to reenact his search history? Had I turned into a jealous psycho overnight?

When he was logged in and perusing the search history, something caught my eye. There, nestled between college books and college boobs, was the name of an old girlfriend.

Shit. Just. Got. Really. Real.

"Whoa! Scroll back up. What is *that?*" I demanded.

"What is *what?*"

Standing with one arm firmly on my hip, I pointed to the obvious. "THAT! Why were you looking her up? And college boobs?"

I stormed from the room before a single syllable could fall from his pie hole.

The two of us had built a relationship on trust and communication. In my premenstrual mind, this was a total derailment. If he had been craving someone younger, all he had to do was say the word. I was a grown adult who kept my big girl panties on at all times—whether they were in a bunch or not.

A few hours and a bazillion tears later, I made my way to bed. I did not get under the covers. I brought my own blanket for this very special occasion. Since day one, we swore to never go to bed angry at each other. It was our pact. But I had no intention of caving in and letting this one simply blow over. He was not about to receive a free pass for screwing up. Curled up in a ball, as close to the edge as possible, I buried my head in the pillows and pretended to sleep. I was nearly tossed overboard when he finally crawled into bed next to me.

"Are you sleeping?" he whispered, somewhere near the back of my head.

I tried to play dead.

"Hey. Are you awake?" When I didn't reply, he resorted to gentle tapping—on my freaking cheek. *Who does shit like that?*

Again, I did my best cadaver impersonation.

"I know you're awake. Will you just talk to me? I didn't mean to hurt you." His voice was sincere, but I stood my ground. I was a CPR dummy. Immovable. Without words.

There was heavy sighing followed by endless minutes of back-and-forth rolling. I was married to the fire department's Stop, Drop, and Roll poster child. And he was driving me crazy.

"Can you STOP moving?" I finally screamed.

"I knew you were awake!" He sat upright, and, through the dim moonlight, I could see his finger pointed in my direction. There was a smile on his face.

"This isn't forgiveness! I want you to leave me alone. I want you to stop rolling all around the bed. And I never, ever, want you to poke me in the cheek again. *Got it?*"

He lay back down and turned away from me. Quiet and motionless.

Over the years I have discovered that there are two kinds of silence: uncomfortable and questionable.

At this point, I was questioning which one of us was the bigger asshole. Me for not allowing him an opportunity to justify his actions and for completely hurting his feelings by breaking our "no going to bed angry" pact? Or him for what had played out earlier that day?

I caved in. "Okay. You have two minutes to explain yourself before I grab my blanket and pillow and head for the couch."

In less than thirty seconds, he rattled off the details of his Internet exploits. An old girlfriend whom he hadn't seen or talked to in years had sent him a friend request on Facebook. Curious to see what she had been doing with her life, he clicked on her profile before ignoring her request. That was the extent of his cyber unfaithfulness, as he called it. As far as college boobs, it was clear that he had been searching for college books. And knowing my husband, he most likely typed in "boobs" erroneously. With boobs shoved squarely in his face, it was hard turning back. I admitted that I would've had the same reaction had I typed in "bright painted balls" instead of "bright painted walls." *Can you imagine?*

We made up before going to sleep that night. Our pact remained intact, and I learned two valuable lessons: 1) honesty and communication really are essential to a healthy marriage, and 2) it's never a bad thing to clear your search history, even when your actions are innocent—or when the temptation of perky, double Ds causes a moment of extreme asshattery.

CRYSTAL PONTI IS THE FOUNDER OF BLUE LOBSTER BOOK CO., A self-publishing boutique. Prior to launching her own business, she worked for and advised some of the largest sites in the world and spent a number of years as a business and marketing planning consultant. She recently served as Managing Editor, Contributing Author, and publisher of the book *The Mother of All Meltdowns*. She blogs at MommiFried, an outlet for her creative writing and a way for her to share her later-in-motherhood experiences with all women and parents. She is a regular contributor to Felicity Huffman's site What The Flicka? and Business2Community, and is also a Huffington Post blogger. When she is not busy consulting, blogging, or writing, she can be found nurturing a beautiful family of five children, a wonderfully Italian husband, and an African-gray parrot with a colorful vocabulary.

Because It's Not a Friday Night Date Unless You Stop at Both Home Depot and Lowe's on Your Way Home

By Meredith Spidel

MAGICAL PERFECTION. MY HUSBAND AND I HAD JUST managed a dinner out *without the kids*. It was one of those rare, blissful moments when you feel like there might somehow, someday be a world outside of poopy diapers and passionate temper tantrums over Goldfish crackers. The power of adult conversation to feed one's soul should not be understated. *It was a good night.*

Leaving the restaurant, I was giddy over our successful flirtation with normalcy. I relaxed into the passenger seat of the minivan, looking forward to sharing more complete sentences with my husband on the way home. I turned toward him, met his gaze, and listened eagerly for the sweet nothings that would surely pour from his mouth at any moment.

It was then that he said, "We need to stop at Home Depot."

I was stunned. Speechless.

"And Lowe's," he added.

I blinked a few times. Was this some sort of new punking-your-date fad that had been on the news while I let *Daniel Tiger* dominate my TV screen for two years straight?

"We're on a date," I protested.

"We need a new refrigerator."

"We're on a date," I tried again.

"You want a new refrigerator." I did—he was right about that. Our current refrigerator was frighteningly losing cooling power by the day.

"Yes, but we don't have to get it tonight."

I then noticed him squirming uncomfortably in his seat.

"I sort of need to pick up some electrical cord and nails."

"NOW?"

"Well, yes ... but-I-really-like-shopping-with-you-it's-fun-to-just-spend-time-with-you." The lameness of his pitiful appeal could be smelled a mile away.

I like spending time with my husband too. I even (sometimes, though rarely) like shopping with him, but in my head, quality date night time includes less large box stores and fewer men in orange aprons.

My husband sensed that he was not yet on firm ground, so he did IT. He played the one card he knew I couldn't argue with, "We have no other time. Doing this when we have the kids with us would stink."

He was right, of course, again. There must have been some phenomenally informative class on shopping with young children that we had missed because we are terrible at running errands with them. We chase our kids through the aisles screaming, "Don't touch that!" Both of us quake at the thought and prefer our children in the padded privacy of our own home.

Truth be told, except on this one most excellent night of the year, our kids are almost always with us. And we did need a new refrigerator.

"Okay," I said, "as long as we're quick about it."

Those. Famous. Last. Words.

As it turns out, there is nothing quick about refrigerator shopping. Nothing at all. When you factor in all the bottom freezers, ice dispensers, and pull-out shelving, things get complicated—*very* complicated. Clerks named Chuck get involved and have surprisingly strong opinions. Suddenly, hours have passed, and it's no longer clear to anyone whether we are actually in Home Depot, Lowe's, or some sort of stainless-steel appliance dream sequence gone horribly wrong.

Finally, it was time to bid Chuck adieu. We had survived our intensive crash-course on refrigeration. Only just. The adventure had ended, the large appliance aisles were abandoned, and thousands upon thousands of product-serial-number-capturing phone pics later, we officially had the best knowledge of the refrigerator market in southeastern Pennsylvania.

It was time to leave and get on with date night. *Which, at this point, meant tiredly scrubbing off my smeared mascara and curling up with earplugs and my beloved word game until dozing off.*

Except—my husband had other plans.

Remember the electrical wire and nails he had mentioned before? He hadn't forgotten about them. His meek, "Hey, I also have to swing by the plumbing section," cued me that I probably had enough time for a bathroom break—a long one, at that.

I won't lie; I definitely felt a little ruggedly boss cutting through the tool section on my way to the bathroom while rocking my date-night outfit. It has to be a cool woman who can navigate Home Depot on a Friday night in heels, right? *Or probably just a fool of a woman, but I was trying hard to pacify myself and see the positives.*

I also took a long moment to feel proud that I even recognized a few of the tools. Being able to identify a steel pipe wrench? My husband landed the whole package when he got me.

Done with the bathroom, it was time to find my husband. I circled the store. And then I circled again. Then I got grouchy and worked to self-soothe by reminding myself of all the awesome steps I was racking up on my Fitbit. *Two thousand, four thousand*—

But the reality was: I was not happy.

I tried calling my husband's cell phone several times. It went directly to voicemail. I thought unkind thoughts in my head. I tried to force myself to think kind ones—*I was not successful.*

Finally, *finally*, I found my guy hanging out by the display of copper pipes and beaming.

"I'm *so* glad they have what I need," he enthused.

I glared at him.

"I'll only be a minute."

The glaring continued.

Honestly, I hadn't been that grouchy about the whole scenario until I saw the pipes. I'm not sure what it was exactly about all that bendy, shiny copper, but I was now over the edge.

It was time to regroup. There must be *something* I could have fun with in the store. Abandoning my husband to his pipe-full bliss, I let my eyes roam over the signs until I found my solution. There was a book section! And even more exciting, it had a bench! *Maybe there was something to this Home Depot after all.*

Mostly there were just a bunch of kids' activities journals and gardening magazines, but we dedicated readers can always find a comfortable home with any type of books. I felt a little bargain-hunting glee brewing inside. I saw price tags with sale stickers on them, and the adrenaline started coursing through my veins. I could look at books *and* possibly save some money? Heck yeah!

Of course, the major bonus at this point was that I could identify the objects I was looking at. Yes, the books definitely had it over the copper pipes in this regard.

So I settled in. I scanned. I perused. I relaxed and was sort of even having fun.

After a while, I wondered if I should look for my husband. It's astounding how time can fly when you settle in with a copy of *How to Homestead With a Smile*, but I was tired and still had dreams of saying hello to my pillow before too long.

I rose to my feet, recommitting to my mission of leaving the store. I was going to find my husband, and we were going home.

As I scanned the massive space, I spotted him at the register checking out. *Humph.* This would make my snippy, "We need to leave NOW" declaration a little less impactful as he was already on his way out the door. Oh well, at least he would be contrite, right?

This, however, was not the case.

As I approached him, he was actually *irritated with me*. "Where were you? I couldn't find you, and I wanted to leave."

Hold. The. Phone.

Was he joking? Was he for real? For the second time that evening, I was stunned speechless. After doing some

By Meredith Spidel

fish-style open-mouth gaping, I said nothing and walked toward the door.

I fumed and stewed and considered a very unseemly public meltdown. And then it hit me: *it was time to laugh about this whole ridiculous evening.*

You cry if you don't laugh. It's true. So I posted, "Because it's not a Friday night date unless you stop at both Home Depot and Lowe's on your way home" on Facebook and made myself chuckle—always a win in my book.

This status update resonated well with others too. As it turns out, I'm not the only spouse who has found themselves committed to late-night lumber shopping. Apparently, it's actually a rather popular pastime with the young-parent crowd. *Who knew?* Bring on that appliance aisle and forget the wine bars.

The more I thought about it, the funnier it got.

I love my husband, and I will always humor his emergency Home Depot runs. I recognize all of his do-it-yourself efforts are for the good of our home and family. If he needs me to tag along, I will, and sometimes I will even do it patiently.

I'm also human. So if you cross my date night, dear Husband, brace yourself. Consider it a win if we end up laughing about it. Consider it an even bigger win if your wife is able to find a few things about the trip that were not only funny, but kind of cool. I really did like that book section. And consider it a HUGE win if, on our next date night, as you're paying the check I'm the one *asking* to stop at Home Depot on the way home.

Hey, I need some mounting tape, which I just happened to see close to those magnificent copper pipes on our last trip.

MEREDITH SPIDEL IS A WRITER, THOUGH SHE'S NOT ENTIRELY sure what that means. If it involves bribing her kids with juice boxes while trying to navigate the beast of social media, she's totally there. Meredith blogs at The Mom of the Year, where she dedicatedly earns her title one epic parenting fail at a time and tries to offer quick, relatable laughs for fellow parents of the world and all their empathizers. She was thrilled to be part of the best-selling anthologies *I Just Want to Pee Alone, I Just Want to Be Alone,* and *You Have Lipstick on Your Teeth.* She has been a staff writer at Aiming Low and has been featured on BlogHer, In the Powder Room, BonBon Break, and Scary Mommy. She remains entirely terrified by crafts, promises to never share any useful household tips, and is fully committed to a less serious look at the world of parenting.

Airplanes, Cell Phones, and Other Things That Crash and Burn

By Andrew S. Delfino

I BLAME THE WRIGHT BROTHERS AND THEIR UNCEASING quest to fly for both my shattered smartphone screen and the fight between my wife and me. I'm not blaming them for actually cracking the glass; that was all me. But if the brothers hadn't successfully flown on December 17, 1903 in Kitty Hawk, North Carolina, there would be no monument for my family and me to visit while on vacation; this also conclusively proves I wouldn't have dropped my smartphone on the granite rock marking the landing of Orville Wright's first flight—heroic in its lack of a meal or even a beverage service. With no Wright brothers' flights, there would be no Wright Brothers National Memorial, so

I would probably have been at the beach instead. Ergo, my phone would still be intact.

My wife has a different perspective. To her, this is just one more example of my inability to be responsible and take proper care of either situations or my possessions— one more item in a long string that stretches back to the beginning of our relationship. While neither of us keeps track of these things—my wife is not at all a shrew—these examples do exist, making up the texture of our one constant and unresolved issue: whether I'm truly as responsible as an adult ought to be.

The broken phone situation wasn't helped by the afternoon heat, nor by our three children tired from a day of playing at the beach. No, I screwed up again, giving my wife another source of stress on what was supposed to be a relaxing vacation with our kids—the biggest summer paradox of all.

I had slipped my phone out of my pocket to take a picture of my first born on the marker of the first flight. In my head, the irony seemed like it'd make for a clever Facebook status update. That was before my phone slipped out of my hand and harshly kissed the granite memorial.

"Dammit," I said a little too loudly as I picked up my phone and saw the spidery cracks that had turned it into a very expensive light mosaic.

"Oooh Daddy!" my daughter said as she looked down from the marker on which she was perched. "What'd you *do* to your phone? Mommy! Daddy broke his phone!"

"It's not broken, sweetie," I said, trying not to yell "Tattle tale!" at my daughter. Both my sunglasses and the blazing afternoon sun made it hard to see anything on my phone's screen. It no longer even looked like a light mosaic, but a remarkably accurate portrait of a black rectangle.

My wife glanced at the screen and took on what I call "The Look." While that might apply to some wives' bedroom eyes, for me The Look is far from sexy. Instead, it means the launch of another one of our fights over how irresponsible I am.

"Not broken, eh?" she said.

Our disagreements invariably follow the same pattern—much like every patchouli-wearing college hippy follows the pattern of eventually graduating, finding a real job, and buying real deodorant:

Step 1: I screw up a situation or break some object that may or may not cost us time or money to fix (e.g. mapping out directions to a campsite, the watch she gave me as an engagement present, a smartphone screen, and so on).

Step 2: My wife finds out and gets upset.

Step 3: I make up an excuse that tries not to blame others, merely explaining why it wasn't entirely my fault—see the Wright brothers' example above.

Step 4: She doesn't give me the silent treatment exactly, but she certainly gives more than one-word answers when she's not upset. The Look appears in Step 4: her eyes stare at me as though she is wondering whether it is too late to trade me in for a husband who is a fully functioning, responsible adult.

Step 5: I fix it as best I can—it almost always gets fixed or at least gets better and rarely does it ever get worse.

Step 6: Eventually she explains why she's mad at me.

Step 7: A week later, we're back to normal, until the next time I relapse like the chubby kid back from fat camp walking by a McDonald's.

At that point, while I was standing in the heat and humidity of the Outer Banks (would it have killed the Wright brothers to invent flight somewhere with shade trees?), we were at Step 2, moving to Step 4, so I wisely avoided cursing out the fathers of modern flight anywhere but in my head. In her frustration, she said nothing, instead taking our son for a walk to the end of the granite markers, down to the farthest marker, number four where Wilbur flew 852 feet— leaving me alone for 1,704 feet with the two girls, ages seven and two, bickering over who would get to climb the next marker first.

I tried not to take out my frustration and anger at myself on the girls by yelling at them. After all, they were only doing what sisters do naturally: fight. Patiently, I broke it up, and we chose to forgo the death march to yet another chunk of rock I couldn't photograph at that moment. I took them both by the hand, and went to check out the model of the cabin the Wright brothers stayed in while they were attempting to recreate the flight of birds, though with much less crapping. The brothers had an ingenious setup for their beds, suspending them high up between the cabin's rafters. Instead of marveling, all I could think of was how their cell phones would probably have cracked if they were to fall out of their pockets while they were in bed. Granted, this made no sense at all, since in 1903 the Outer Banks was definitely a dead zone for airplanes, and more so for 4G data.

Nonetheless, I should have been marveling, but I was stressing about the phone. I'd made yet another mistake that would cost us money. The phone was expensive and not even a year old. Sure, I once read an article about cracked screens giving kids street cred, but I'm in my thirties. I need Hair Club for Men more than I need any props from people who still need their mothers to drive them to the movies. No, the cracked screen was very bad, especially since it struck the raw nerve that is our marriage's primary argument.

During our sixteen years together, these mistakes have led to fights, but eventually most of them became funny stories for my wife and me to laugh about (see #6 above)— like the time right after we were engaged when I bought an airplane ticket to my parents' fortieth-anniversary party without asking her if she wanted to come with me. This forced us to travel separately on our first trip back to California after we moved to Georgia—though that was probably a good thing since I ended up missing my flight (ironically, the Wright brothers cannot be blamed) because I forgot to print my ticket information and got to the airport only thirty minutes before takeoff. I once forgot the fancy watch she gave me in my pants' pocket and sent it through the wash. Three different times. I tried to help her refinish some dining room chairs and actually sanded off all the wood stain she had painstakingly applied over the weekend. One time, I said I would take care of packing the camping equipment and forgot pillows and tent stakes, and we had to move the minivan to block the wind so the tent didn't fly away. Simple mistakes, all of them, made funny by time and distance.

Since we've had kids, and I've become a stay-at-home father, these incidents continue to bother her. Amazingly, I have matured over the years, and I've never been completely irresponsible or reckless while taking care of the children. Mostly. Sure, I didn't notice our son feed his little sister a sample-sized tube of toothpaste once, but what parent doesn't have a toothpaste-eating story? Usually my mistakes do not involve other people, but rather objects or situations like three speeding tickets from the same photo-radar camera. (In my defense, they artificially lower the speed limit on that street to ten miles per hour, and I was only going twenty-five. I was basically ticketed for driving as safely as I could without actually getting out and pushing my car.)

So cracking my phone at the Wright Brothers Memorial was not surprising, even though it was obviously still too soon to laugh about it.

As my seven-year-old and I talked about the Wright brothers' cabin and tried to keep the toddler from jumping on the beds, my wife and son rejoined us.

"I'm sorry I dropped my phone," I said to her, as we looked back into a time where there were no cell phones but probably plenty of marital discord. "It was an accident."

"How much is this 'accident' going to cost us?" she asked, neatly sidestepping my excuse.

"You've never dropped your phone?" I asked.

"Only once," she said. "Even so, I take better care of my phone than you take care of yours."

Our seven-year-old overheard us, as did every visitor nearby. An elderly grandmother walked away suddenly, as though she didn't have much longer to live and urgently needed to go see other parts of the memorial. Our daughter inquired as to whether my phone was broken-broken or whether she could still play Dragonbox on it. She'd seen enough boring stuff like the dawn of manned flight and wanted to play some games.

I pulled out my phone and, in the shade of the cabin, saw that it still worked—fissured screen and all.

"No, it isn't broken-broken, but the screen is cracked," I said, looking my wife in the eyes. "But when we get home, I'm sure we can get it fixed for less than a new phone costs."

My wife's eyes softened a little, and The Look faded. Inwardly, I rejoiced that we'd tentatively moved on to Step 5. Later, on the drive back to the beach house we'd rented with friends, she explained how frustrating it is to constantly have to pay to fix mistakes that could be avoided if I just took better care of my things. I could've objected to the word "constantly," but I had just realized that I had forgotten to put the gas cap back on and close the fuel door when we filled up five minutes earlier. Wisely, I said nothing, eager to reach the peace of Step 7.

They say that over a marriage, you may have thousands of fights, but you are really just having the same one over and over and over again. That certainly feels true for my wife and me. Instead of getting upset about this, perhaps there could be a bright side: my wife will have the good fortune to witness all of the other messes that my lack of responsible foresight is sure to get us into. We've probably got at least forty more years of my adventures. Most of them, I hope, will be as easy to fix as a cracked phone screen. I dread the few that may be as difficult to solve as manned flight, like those goddamn Wrights did—and, for that, they still owe me a new phone.

ANDREW S. DELFINO IS PRIMARILY A STAY-AT-HOME DAD AND humor blogger who also teaches writing part-time to college students. After listening to his three (soon to be four) kids have temper tantrums whenever he asks them to do something, he can then go to work and listen to bigger kids have temper tantrums whenever he asks them to write something. While he doesn't mind being called an asshole, he hates being asked if he's babysitting when he's out with his kids. You can read more of his parenting stories at Almost Coherent Parent.

Ham, Tears, and One Toilet: A Mexican Tale

By Kimberly Morand

MY TWENTY-FIFTH BIRTHDAY SNUCK UP ON ME AS swiftly as the back of my dad's hand when he caught me artfully gluing dog hair to my little brother's upper lip. He'd always threatened that one day he'd knock me into next Tuesday if I kept doing terrible things to my brother. I never believed him until I woke up one Tuesday fourteen years later wondering, "Where in the hell did time go?"

Twenty-five isn't as exciting as sweet sixteen or drunk twenty-one. It's the realization that you've lived for a quarter of a century and that every birthday card from hereafter will be about sagging tits and how many candles closer you are to actually burning down a house. It can be a celebratory day of how far you've come and how far you've yet to go, or conversely, it can be one of the most depressing days of your life. It might be a day that you spend wishing you had taken college more seriously and strategically planning a quaint living arrangement in your parents' basement to accommodate your growing family of cats.

For me, turning twenty-five meant Mexico.

"I hope you bought travelers insurance. It's hurricane season," my dad grumbled as I flashed him the two plane tickets that my husband had bought for my birthday.

I elbowed Shawn in the side. "Of course he did." I looked at him. "Right?"

"No."

"Seriously?" I asked.

"What are the chances of that happening?"

"Probably as high as my daughter slamming the patio door on her hand. You know, the same patio door that I've been repeatedly telling everyone you've been 'too busy' to take care of," my dad said bitterly.

"Honey, you *have* to purchase it," I said to my husband. "It would give me peace of mind just knowing that it would at least cover part of our expenses if—"

"Peace of mind? I'll give you a *piece* of mind. There will be such a continuous onslaught of fruity drinks that if something were to happen, you wouldn't even know it."

"Or feel it for that matter," said my dad. "Unlike the pain she'll undoubtedly experience when her severed fingers are stuck in the patio door that I told you to fix."

"Jesus," Shawn said sharply.

"Jesus has nothing to do with it, you heathen."

"You better get the hurricane insurance," I insisted.

"Nope."

"I'm telling you, Shawn, if something happens—"

"Nope."

I channeled my dad from the days of my youth, "If something happens, I'll shove my foot so far up your ass that I'll be able to tickle your tonsils with my toenails."

"You tell him, Kimbers," my dad encouraged.

"Don't worry," Shawn said with conviction. "Nothing is going to happen."

Mexico welcomed us with gusts of warm breezes that masked the intensity of the blazing sun. The ocean's gentle waves nipped at the heels of newly married couples walking along the shoreline, and upbeat Latin music streaming through speakers secured to tiki huts made the atmosphere feel both relaxed and charged for a good time. I flopped myself onto a lounge chair and closed my eyes. This was a far cry from the threatening weather I'd been worried about.

I was startled when ice-cold drops splashed onto my stomach. I looked up to see Shawn standing over me, holding two large glasses filled to the rim with a slushy concoction of booze and artificial flavoring. He was too busy staring to his left to notice the cold condensation dripping from the glasses onto his lovely wife.

"Check the set on that guy," he chuckled.

Following his gaze, I was revolted yet oddly mesmerized by a left testicle so large it couldn't be contained in the small blue Speedo that a "drunken Dutchman" was wearing. It slapped against his inner thigh as he struggled to put one foot in front of the other in the sand. He saw us staring and pretended to tip the invisible glass he was holding in our direction—a friendly toast. He staggered off to the bar where the bartender politely told him to "tuck it in" before he sat on a stool.

"If you keep drinking like that, by the end of this trip he won't be the only one leaving sack tracks on everything. You two are kindred spirits. The most hairy pair of peas in a pod," I joked.

My husband wasn't the only one drinking. The hotel waiters made sure my glass was never empty. I drank until I forgot that I had limbs and dignity—catching Frisbees with my throat and giving high fives to the men using urinals. By the end of the evening, I had acquired a sombrero and a replica shotgun, both of which my husband had to hold for me while I painted the ground outside the lobby a peculiar shade of purple.

"Now that is sidewalk art *a la carte*," I said as I wiped my chin.

I was still drunk when the hammering outside of our patio door woke me up early the next morning. I rolled toward Shawn, only to discover that his mouth was wide open and drier than a geriatric hooker. I stuck my finger just far enough down his throat to make him gag.

"What?" he snarled as he punched my hand away.

"Oh, I was just thinking."

"Thinking of what?"

"Of how awesome it would be if you slept with your mouth shut."

"You woke me up to tell me that my breath stinks? Is it that bad?"

"If it wasn't that bad, how do you explain the hazmat team outside nailing car deodorizers to the walls?"

He got up and whipped open the patio door. Over his shoulder, I could see the sun being suffocated by thick, grey, ominous clouds and that a host of hotel staff was busy nailing boards over windows. "Wilma!" one shouted.

"Did I tell everyone that my name is Wilma? And did I fuck up all those windows last night?" I asked.

"Wilma!" the hotel worker said again. "*Hurricane* Wilma."

I clenched my jaw, and my husband instinctively protected his groin with an accent pillow.

"What are the chances of that happening?" I mimicked. "What are the chances, eh? We don't need insurance. Meh. Meh. Meh. You know what? You're an asshole."

Shortly afterwards, a hotel employee guided us to a room to be shared with six other people. He handed us two ham sandwiches to tide us over until the storm passed and cackled quietly as he shut the door behind him.

Shawn lifted a black duffle bag and laid it on the dresser.

"You brought food from the restaurant? Thank goodness!" an older woman said with delight.

"Better," he replied as he started to empty the contents—socks upon socks and a large number of washcloths.

"I don't get it," said the woman.

The man with the five-o'clock shadow perked up, "Is that what I think it is carefully tucked inside?"

My husband nodded as he pulled out the bottles of beer that he had taken from our room fridge. "Let's party, bitches."

The women in the room collectively sighed, and I settled down on our new accommodation, a humble mattress that had been lovingly placed on the floor in front of the bathroom.

The world looked incredibly small as the waves reached out from the ocean like a giant's hand, grasping anything they could before receding. Our patio window bowed in and out with the forceful winds that had already begun to peel the paint off the villas and lift the thatch roofs off the tiki huts. Only four walls and one fragile window separated us from Wilma. We were at her mercy, and the ham sandwiches were our only source of nourishment.

Shawn's best action-hero tone was marred by his slurred words. "Here's the plan. I can't swim, so if the waves start coming our way, I'm going to bust down the closet door and float on top of it."

"Titanic."

"Kind of. You can swim, so if I need to, I can let go of you with a clean conscience."

"Oh man. I've got to take a shit," one of our roomies said suddenly, as he held his stomach and ran to the bathroom. Oh, the inhumane noises that began to rumble beyond the door and into our room. In minutes, there was a line of angry intestines outside the bathroom door, begging for a turn to ride the thunder bucket. The bowel contractions of each of us were five minutes apart, and some of us were crowning.

"What are the chances? What are the chances of food poisoning?" I mocked as Shawn rocked back and forth in the fetal position. "A flying taco is going to kill me. How's that for a clean conscience?"

Wilma was unrelenting. She sat above the Mayan Riviera for two days, causing mass destruction, and only began to tire out on the third day. We wanted to break free, like my sister's pet bird that I once let out the back door for shitting on my face, but as the hotel staff instructed us, we waited in our room until we had permission to leave.

"Do you hear that?" asked the woman who had anxiously sweated through three flowered shirts. "It sounds like someone is outside the door!" She jumped up and looked through the peephole. "Oh my god! Nuts!"

"Is it that bad out there?" I asked, running to her side. I unlatched the door cautiously and poked my head out. And there they were—two literal nuts hanging out of a familiar blue Speedo. The drunken Dutchman was busy squeegee-ing the hallway floor. When he saw us, he tried to stand up, but failed. Then he said, "Hey! Tequila!"

And so it went.

Four days later, we boarded a plane back to Canada. Since the great poop-a-looza in our hotel room, I'd had barely the stomach to eat a single thing. I was now famished. The flight attendant came down the aisle, handing each passenger a sandwich and cookies. I had never been so excited about an airplane meal. As I unwrapped the cellophane package, I praised Jesus for the untainted food I was about to put in my mouth.

"Babe, it's a ham sandwich," my husband warned.

And I cried.

Almost ten years after Wilma, I find myself standing back on a balcony in the Mayan Riviera during hurricane season. The palm trees are bending with the ferocious winds, and the drunks below are taunting the skies for more. The hotel room door slams shut, and I say to my husband, "You're an asshole. I don't know how you ever talked me into coming back here. Because what are the chances of it happening again, Shawn?"

"Don't worry. I got insurance this time," he replies, shaking a box of anti-diarrheal medicine and a turkey sandwich.

KIMBERLY MORAND IS A MOM, WIFE, NURSE, MENTAL HEALTH advocate, and full-time chocolate hater. When she's not busy pretending to look busy, she's writing for *SZ Magazine, Anchor: Conquering Depression, Bipolar, and Anxiety.* Kimberly was the first Canadian member to join the talented cast of the 2014 Listen to Your Mother Show: Metro Detroit. Her work can also be found in

The Good Mother Myth: Redefining Motherhood to Fit Reality. She fears spiders, public restrooms, and your mom's cooking.

Shitter

By Jonathon Floyd

THE DYNAMIC OF THE FIGHTS BETWEEN MY WIFE AND me has completely changed over the years. As our relationship became more serious, so did the fights. They morphed from cutesy, eighth-gradish, and almost fun into something completely different. Harsh words. Irrational. Fueled by sleep deprivation. We'd say anything to win. It was an ongoing power struggle. The only common denominator: both types were a complete waste of time. Yet the evolution of our fights, from courting through kids, is fascinating as shit.

I remember when my future wife and I started dating. Our fights were highly entertaining. I looked forward to them, actually. They were never over anything serious. I mean, how much responsibility did we have back then compared to now? None. The fights were over things like:

"I haven't seen you at all in the last week!"

"You work too much!"

"Why are you going to that party when we could be together?"

Or:

"Why do you still have your ex's number in your phone?"

One question would lead to the volume getting turned way up, and a loud, ridiculous fight would ensue—until one of us would have enough and say, "I'm sorry baby," followed by a simple touch on the leg or the neck. And then—cue the really hot make-up sex in a totally inappropriate place! It would always happen exactly where we were at the time. A parking lot. A driveway. The kitchen. It didn't matter. Like I said, fights were fun.

Ding-dong went the wedding bells. Along came marriage mixed with a simultaneous whole-house renovation. Needless to say, our stress levels increased—and so did the fights. But they were still silly. We never lived together before getting hitched. I remember our first night together at home after the honeymoon. I looked at her like, "Don't you have someplace to go?" We had to learn to tolerate and accept each other's idiosyncrasies—like me not making the bed in the morning or not closing the bathroom door when I pooped. Of course, she was perfect. There were the typical arguments over paint colors, whether to put a dirt berm in the front yard, tile versus hardwood—you know, real-life, hard-hitting arguments. Then, the baby talk started. Although I was scared shitless, I felt the need to spread my seed, and just like that, she was pregnant.

Maybe I read too much on the Internet, but I refused to argue while she was carrying our child. I was convinced the baby would be born a crack head with post-traumatic stress disorder and have no hopes of getting into a good college. Pregnancy was a great time for us. We were sweet to each other and the baby. I loved whispering into her belly. There was always music playing. We wanted to make sure our child was well-cultured by the time he hit the streets. Together, we pigged out at buffets, planned our hospital playlist, took natural child birthing classes, and talked endlessly about all the possibilities for our new addition. Who would he look like? Would he be a carny or a president? We both agreed, as long as he was healthy, we didn't care if he was a Martian.

There was one teensy, weensy little argument during the pregnancy. We saved it until the very end, literally while she was writhing on the table in hard labor. We had agreed that no matter how much she begged, she would not have an epidural. It was her wish to have the baby without drugs. Her body. Her rules. I nervously agreed that if medical intervention was not necessary, I would help her keep that promise to herself and the baby.

Fast forward to her clawing my arm off while on the delivery table—

Now she's begging for an epidural! My head was spinning. We were all alone in the delivery room. She was screaming in pain. I felt helpless! I grabbed my phone with the free hand that wasn't being mauled and texted our birth coach for advice.

Just then she caught a glimpse of me, and, in her best Linda Blair from *The Exorcist* voice, growled, "Put down that fucking phone!"

I pushed send and within seconds received the response, "She's in transition. The baby's almost here!" Of course, "Da Coach" was right. Within thirty minutes, our little buddy was introduced to the world. I cried more than he did. After almost two days in the hospital, our little family headed home. I remembered the one piece of advice every parent had given us: "Sleep as much as possible before the baby's born, because you're never going to sleep again." Yeah right, I thought.

You know the old saying about never discussing politics or religion in polite company? Well, after the baby, I soon learned, "Never discuss money or parenting styles in exhausted company." And discussing both at the same time—well, you're just asking for a shit-show. Here's an example:

I stagger down to the kitchen in an attempt to assist Wifey with breakfast. I hear the clothes washer chugging away downstairs.

Without thinking, I simply ask, "Are you washing another load of diapers? I wonder if all the water we're using is worth the savings on disposables?"

You'd think I just lit a firecracker in her snatch. But as much as she wanted to "light me up," there was the baby, sitting in the high chair, watching our every move. Thus, the very reason our fights have evolved into something completely different.

Wifey and I have a standing agreement. Do not argue in front of the kids. There are two now. So here's the new anatomy of our fights, I mean debates. One of us pushes the other's automatic piss-me-off buzzer. Again, it's usually over money or parenting. Next follows the awkward silence. Take a deep breath. And then, through clenched teeth, politely attempt to make your point without tipping off the youngster. We spell a lot of words like, "You're being a complete A-S-S hole!"

If we can't solve the issue or at least shut our mouths within a few minutes, I usually leave to "go get groceries." That's code for *I go driving in hopes that cooler heads prevail.* But usually it means we just switch to an all-out text war. My phone's buzzing by the time I've made it down the street, so I pull over and continue our digital debate. I've even stopped at the store to buy a pen and paper, scribbled a multi-page rant, and passed it off to her as I walk in and grab the baby with a huge smile on my face. As the kids get older, they'll get wiser. But for now, we choose not to let them witness Mommy and Daddy acting like complete idiots, not to mention programming them for future reference as they grow up. Remember, like it or not, we're all truly products of our parents.

When it comes to our temper tantrums, the more things change, the more things stay the same. Throughout all these years, no matter how silly or how serious the premise was, our fights have always been about the same things: mutual respect, appreciation and recognition for each other's hard work and sacrifices, and trying to maintain some semblance of our former selves. Our marriage is, and will always be, a work in progress. With each debate, we get a little better and little smarter at communicating with each other. I know that I need to make eye contact and pay attention while my wife is speaking to me. Texting during our discussion is still a big no-no. She understands that I need at least twenty minutes and two cups of coffee before she says anything other than, "Good morning." And although my solo-dad routine with the kids isn't exactly the same as her routine with them, I still manage to keep them happy and alive.

It's all about compromise. And the dirty make-up sex still occurs. It just happens two weeks after the fight in the accidental two minutes we have alone together. Well, pending there are no kids crying in their rooms, reminding me of how I got myself into this mess in the first place. That's a real boner-killer.

CHICAGO-ISH, ILLINOIS. AGE FORTY. SHIFT WORKER. WRITER. Artist. Millionaire entrepreneur. Famous drummer. Comedic genius. Ex-porn star. Compulsive liar. Jonathon Floyd studied creative writing in Mrs. Delrose's third-grade English class. He began his formal writing career on a dare, penning three-hundred-sixty-five consecutive daily Facebook posts describing his first year through the eyes of a new dad. From those posts, his blog, One Funny Daddy, was born. Although Jonathon does not consider himself a blogger or writer, he still manages to bang out daily posts on social media sites from an iPhone in his upstairs bathroom.

The Great Christmas Card Incident of Ought Six

By Sarah del Rio

THERE COMES A POINT IN EVERY MARRIAGE WHEN A dizzying moment of clarity occurs, and we realize there are some things our spouses just *Will Not Do*.

This rude awakening doesn't happen immediately. After all, the warm and intoxicating rays of the honeymoon phase usually keep newlyweds in a prolonged state of sleepy, sated denial. (I blame it on the gettin' some.) Still, all good things come to an end, and even the most passionate and oversexed couple cannot thwart the resolute passage of time. Try as we might to prevent it, the first blush of marriage always and inevitably fades.

And that, my friends, is when certain realities start to hit home.

"You know what? Now that I think about it, I'm pretty sure my wife has never gassed up her own car. Her ... own ... car."

"My husband refuses to change the Diaper Genie because 'the smell makes him puke.' I guess he thinks I find it just delectable."

"We have Alamo-style standoffs to see who'll give in and put away the dishes first. I'm sure you can guess which one of us is Texas."

The particulars of the Will Not Do phenomenon differ from person to person. Myself? I never shovel the driveway. I don't rake the leaves, and I don't mow the lawn. And I will not get on a ladder for any reason. If the zombie apocalypse happened and there was a decaying corpse stuck in my rain gutter, I'd be all, "Welp, that sucks," right before doing absolutely nothing about it.

Above all else, I absolutely refuse to deal with bugs. For real. I won't. If there is a bug within a half-mile radius of me, you can bet I'm fully aware of its existence and have already called upon my husband to dispatch it with extreme prejudice (a flip-flop and a piece of toilet paper).

Trust.

Before you rush to judgment, don't forget that my husband has his very own and very extensive Will Not Do list. For example, he is completely incapable of scheduling or attending a playdate. He has an almost visceral aversion to the tedious intricacies of school and church. He is polite to a fault, yet somehow can never find the time to write a thank-you note. He does not *répondez s'il vous plaît*.

Holidays aren't his thing, either—particularly the ones that require a lot of effort.

Christmas, for example.

I'm going to get sexist for a minute and say that men are just generally pretty useless at Christmas. Sure, they'll do *some* stuff. They'll put up the outdoor lights. They'll help maneuver Christmas trees into the house. They'll go out into the yard and set up those hideous Christmas inflatables that look like deformed snow globes or a creepy Santa riding a motorcycle.

And—those are the Christmas contributions of men. End of list.

Conversely, here's just a *short* list of what women do:

Buy ALL the presents. Oh, and I do mean *all* the presents. Presents for the husband's parents? Check. Presents for the husband's friends? Check. Presents for the husband's co-workers, some of whom we've never even met? Check. Gee, I hope they like wine and cheese baskets! Because that's the completely thoughtless gift they're all getting.

Wrap the presents. Ever had the worst backache in the world? No? Want to try it? Simply wrap dozens upon dozens of gifts in one sitting, all while hunkered down on the floor amidst a humongous mess of wrapping paper, gift bags, tissue paper, decorative bows, tape, and seven pairs of scissors that are never anywhere to be found when you need them. (Pro tip: they're always under a butt cheek.)

Send the Christmas cards. In this day and age of international families, Internet friends, global workplaces, and the politically correct etiquette of including everyone in everything, Christmas card lists are now literally hundreds of thousands of miles long. And who chooses and buys the Christmas cards? Who stuffs, seals, and stamps the envelopes? Who addresses them and takes them to the post office? Not men.

Decorate the house. First, we brave the basement or other gross, bug-filled storage space in order to dig out the metric ton of Christmas decorations we've collected over the years. Then, we unwrap every single decoration, leaving the entire house awash in discarded bubble wrap and ancient newspaper. Last, we place, adjust, and readjust each item 2,938,472,934 times in an attempt to keep the house from looking like a Home Goods holiday clearance shelf threw up in it. (Impossible.)

Plan and prepare the Christmas meals. Choose recipes. Acquire groceries. Polish silverware. Bust out the good china that can't be run through the dishwasher. Cook. Bake. Plate. Serve. Watch everyone finish eating in fifteen seconds. Clean up leftovers while the entire family hangs out in the living room, burping and snoring their way through the digestive process. Develop butt-loads of resentment and an ulcer.

Obviously the list goes on (and on), but I think you get the point.

Unfortunately, when I was a newlywed, I did not fully realize just how many Christmas responsibilities were on my husband's Will Not Do list. After all, we'd only been married for five months when our very first Christmas together rolled around, and the gettin' some was still quite frequent. Our emotions were still very much located in our underpants regions. Which is why when I started asking my husband to help out with Christmas tasks, and he started responding with a million-and-one excuses for why he'd love to but couldn't possibly, I hitched up my big girl panties and just dealt with it. You know. Because sex.

But things came to a head regarding the Christmas cards.

For whatever reason, I had it in my mind that Christmas cards from two people should be signed by both parties. (How stupid and naïve I was then.) Yet at the same time, I understood that my husband was incredibly busy with work and school, so I thought I'd do him a humongous favor and take care of 99 percent of the job.

I chose the cards. I wrote short, friendly notes inside of the cards. I signed my name to the cards. I enclosed photographs in the cards. I addressed the envelopes. I put stamps on the envelopes. I placed the envelopes in neat stacks on the table. I did *everything* that needed to be done for this particular holiday task to be Mission: Completed—everything except sign my husband's name. That was the one part he needed to do.

So I waited.

And waited.

And waited.

Thinking that maybe he'd just forgotten, I reminded him. Nothing happened. I reminded him again. I was assured that he would get to it. He didn't. I reminded him a third, fourth, and seventeenth time. It was starting to get awfully close to Christmas, and the cards were still naked of his signature. And one night after dinner, I snapped.

I mean it. I SNAPPED.

I called my husband to the carpet for his endless stream of false Christmas card-signing promises. I yelled at him about his complete lack of interest in making our first Christmas together a holly jolly experience. I cried and sobbed about how hard I'd been working to stay on top of the holidays. No thanks to him.

Then I shouted, "THIS ISN'T WORKING!"

And time stopped.

Of course, what I meant was that the balance of our Christmas responsibilities was neither fair nor equitable. Of course, what I meant was that the bottleneck in our Christmas card assembly line was threatening to endanger the whole operation. Of course, what I meant was that I couldn't believe I was getting so upset about something so ridiculous and unimportant.

But what my husband heard?

Was that I wanted a divorce. Over Christmas cards.

He stood up from the dining room table so violently that the chair toppled over backwards. He stomped into our little kitchen and threw something in the plastic wastebasket with such force that the wastebasket smacked up against the kitchen wall and cracked down the middle. Then with the lame, completely transparent excuse that he "now needed to go buy a new wastebasket," he grabbed his jacket, stormed out the door, and drove away.

He was gone for hours.

When my husband finally came home (in his defense, he did actually have a new wastebasket), he had managed to calm down a little bit, but was still obviously distressed and had a face like a slapped cat. So I walked him gently over to our couch, sat him down, and asked him why on earth he had gotten so upset and left the house in such a state.

At which point he looked at me like I was a total moron and cried out in disbelief, "What the hell are you talking about? You just told me you wanted a divorce!"

I hadn't, of course. But that's what he'd understood. When I realized this, I quickly reassured him that he'd taken my words out of context and that I absolutely did not want a divorce. That I loved him more than life itself. That I wouldn't have married him if I weren't in it to win it. Of course, the entire time I was saying all this stuff, I was also biting through the corner of my lip to keep from laughing in his stupid, adorable face.

But let's fast forward to now. As you might have guessed, my husband and I did not in fact split up over what shall be forever known as The Great Christmas Card Incident of Ought Six. Of course we still have our Will Not Do lists, but we are now considerably more familiar with them than when we first got hitched, which I find especially impressive given how much longer they've grown since the birth of our son. (I do nothing to contribute to our son's physical education. My husband will not read the *Little House* books at bedtime.) The short of the long is this: despite our extensive Will Not Do lists, my husband and I have spent eight long and happy years together. And you know what? We plan on hanging in there for quite a few more.

At least until the zombie apocalypse forces the gutter-cleaning issue.

A CORPORATE REFUGEE WITH ABSOLUTELY NO FORMAL TRAINING in English, journalism, or writing of any kind, Sarah del Rio still manages to find work as a freelance writer and editor. In addition to raising her very precocious son, Sarah also writes the award-winning comedy blog est. 1975, is a regular writer for BLUNTmoms, and has been featured on Scary Mommy and In the Powder Room.

Melted Dreams

By Sarah Cottrell

WHEN MY HUSBAND AND I GOT MARRIED, WE RECITED generic vows to love, honor, and cherish through sickness and health and some other unrealistic stuff. We held hands and gazed into each other's eyes with high hopes of not screwing up over the next seventyish years.

With the benefit of hindsight, and after suffering through the comedic skirmishes of two pregnancies, I have come to wonder if perhaps our vows ought to have included the following addendums:

The husband vows to give the wife generous freedom to be a crazy goon during pregnancy.

The husband vows to back the hell off all baked goods, frozen desserts, and extra helpings of carbs during pregnancy.

The husband shall vow to admit his wrongness (however real or merely imagined by the wife) during pregnancy.

Although this may appear on the surface to benefit only the wife and to be sorely unfair toward the poor husband, I assure you it is as close to fair as fair can get. The wife has to grow a child through hormone-fueled insanity and then birth it, after all. And by the time she has accomplished this truly miraculous feat of nature, her body is a freak-show mess.

So really, the husband is getting off easy.

While we were still young and fresh, we made all of the commitments a couple could make in order to ensure that breaking up would be nearly impossible. We got mortgaged, married, and knocked up. We had stars in our eyes. We had registries for everything. We had *all* the answers for success in marriage and parenthood because we read some *How-To* books.

During our first pregnancy, I had morning sickness all day and night. I was grouchy and huffy. My skin was splotchy, my body bloated, my hair dried, and my nerves frazzled. My husband was sweet and supportive through this epic journey toward parenthood. That Sainted man. He even had empathy cravings for the *same* things I craved, namely pastries and ice cream.

Everything was going at a steady pace until I turned the corner of the first trimester and became a nightmare of emotions. I cried *all the time*. One day while I was rummaging through the kitchen pantry in desperate search of a brownie or chocolate or *something*, I started sobbing because there were no freshly baked cookies in the cookie jar.

Also, there was no cookie jar.

My husband (who, by the way, was minding his own business) wandered into the kitchen and was immediately assaulted by a barrage of remarkably irrational questions and accusations sputtering from my cookie-less mouth.

Me: "What the hell kind of mother doesn't have cookies on her kitchen counter? And we don't even have a cookie jar! And what the fuck ... I don't have aprons or anything. I can't even cook! I just eat crap. I can't figure out how to read a fucking recipe right! What the hell is a *roux?* I'm the worst mother already!"

Him: "Oh my god, are you serious?"

Me: "... sniff ... sniff ... sniff ... you jerk!"

Admittedly, I was a tad bit out of control, but it really wasn't my fault. I had enough hormones running through my system to potentially poison a grown man. My sanity was totally checked out for the remaining months of my pregnancy. To make matters worse, my emotions were trigger happy and ready to erupt into tear-jerky, snot-flowing attacks at any moment.

AT&T commercial connecting long-lost family members? Tears and gasping sighs.

My husband drank coffee *in front of me?* Tears and gasping sighs.

I ripped the seat of my pants when I sat down? Tears and gasping sighs.

I could easily have become a ridiculous reality show on Bravo. Honestly, I'm a little surprised at myself that I willingly went through all of this a second time a few years later.

But for all the drama and silliness that my wild emotions caused my poor husband and me, nothing would prepare us for the day we fought over ice cream. At the time, it was the most serious crime against pregnant humanity. For a split second, I was ready to divorce my jerk husband.

It was a Saturday night. I was on my ninth trip to the kitchen for more food things to shove into my mouth. I was eating for two, you know. I had already polished off a plate of sweet potato gnocchi with a lovely tomato-bacon sauce. I had eaten two servings of garlic bread and had the audacity to pick at my husband's plate *while he was still eating.* I ate handfuls of chocolate-covered almonds, and I was three snacks away from looking for my evening bowl of ice cream.

I waddled into the kitchen and opened the freezer door. There it was: my favorite flavor of frozen comfort, chocolate salted-caramel. A whole, unopened pint. I pulled it out and grabbed a spoon. After one delicious, heavenly bite, the phone rang. I put the ice cream away and waddled into the living room.

The night progressed like every Saturday night in those expectant months. My husband rubbed my feet. I complained about every single ache and craving. We daydreamed about names and facial features. At some point,

I remembered that I had my favorite ice cream waiting for me in the freezer.

I waddled back into the kitchen and opened the freezer door. The ice cream was gone. Wait. *The ice cream was gone?* THE ICE CREAM WAS GONE!

Me: "THE ICE CREAM IS GONE? YOU ATE MY ICE CREAM!"

Him: "Huh?"

Me: "I knew it! You selfish bastard! You couldn't let me have JUST ONE indulgent thing to my fat, pregnant self, could you?"

Him: "Honey, what the hell are you shouting about?"

Me: "Oh, I'm not even shouting yet, you big fat jerk! YOU ATE MY GODDAMN ICE CREAM!"

Him: "Oh Jesus. I did not eat your goddamn ice cream. Have you lost your mind? You already ate enough food to feed an army, and *now* you're bitching about ice cream?"

Me: "Who says that shit to a pregnant woman? I'm a fucking vessel of life and beauty, you dick wad!"

Him: "Alright, listen. I did not eat your damn ice cream. Now calm the hell down, and I'll run to the store and buy you a new pint."

Me: *(huffing indignantly)* "Damn right you will!"

Him: *(rolling his eyes, grabbing car keys, leaving for the store)*

Me: *(muttering to myself because I'm obviously on a roll here)* "What the hell kind of jerk face does that? Seriously? I'm carrying the man's child for god's sake. He can't leave me some fucking ice cream ... Ohhh shit!"

At this point in the story, I'm fairly sure that my poor husband was driving ten miles per hour below the speed limit just to spite me. He was probably still arguing with me in his head. I'm sure he was being more honest in his thought bubbles about my pregnancy-induced lunacy than he ever would have dared to my face.

Meanwhile, back in my kitchen, I had just discovered that no one had eaten the ice cream. I had distractedly stuffed it into the breadbox, where it had melted all over a jar of peanut butter and an empty plastic bread bag.

My husband pulled into the driveway about twenty minutes later with a new pint of chocolate salted-caramel ice cream. For a moment, I contemplated eating the melted gloppy mess in my breadbox to save face, but honestly, I was too tired and ready to burst into tears of embarrassment.

When my husband came into the kitchen and saw the mess, he gave me a blank look and said, "Huh. Well look at that."

I let him eat the new pint. I didn't even try to steal a bite.

SARAH COTTRELL LIVES IN MAINE WITH HER BOAT-BUILDER husband and two loud boys. She blogs at the Bangor Daily News under the name Housewife Plus. In 2012, Sarah earned her MFA and since then she has been featured on BlogHer, In the Powder Room, Mamalode, Mamapedia, Scary Mommy, and more.

Que Pasa, Baby Monkey?

By Lisa Petty

LIKE MANY PEOPLE, I HAD A STARTER MARRIAGE—YOU know, that cute little legal promise you make when you're in your twenties and really not that smart. Sure, you're in love, but you don't exactly think about things like what you actually have in common or how you would co-parent. Unlike most people, my starter marriage was with Ricky Ricardo. Actually, he didn't play the bongos, and he wasn't *the* Ricky Ricardo, as I would have had to dig him up to marry him. My ex-husband was and is (it's not like he became Irish after we separated) a Cuban American. He moved to the United States when he was a preschooler, but he grew up in a home where only Spanish was spoken, and he went to school in a part of Miami that might as well require a passport for entry. So as you can probably imagine, there was a series of unfortunate misunderstandings. All that was missing was bright red hair and a rousing rendition of "Babalu."

The first misunderstanding occurred because I was talking to his mother on the phone. We weren't married yet, and I lived in a tiny, icky apartment in Miami (surprise!) with my Ricky. His mom called *constantly*, and if you have ever read my blog or know me in person, you know I hate the phone even when I'm talking to people who speak English. Make me use my high-school Spanish, and I really hate the phone. So one day while I was speaking Spanish to my future mother-in-law, she asked me if her son was *guapo contigo*.

I said, *"sí,"* because I thought *guapo* meant handsome. And it does—in Spain, not in Cuba.

"Did you tell my mom I hit you?" my young Cubano asked later that day.

"I don't know what I told your mom," I answered truthfully. I came to find out that *guapo* means machismo or rough in Cuban Spanish. Who knew? And why on earth would a boy's mama ask his girlfriend if the boy was abusing her? That's just a weird fricking question. No wonder I was confused.

A couple of years after that, I married my Ricky, and we went on a romantic honeymoon to Disney World. Yes, Disney World. One night, way before cell phones with cameras existed, my husband decided to set up his old-school camera (it used actual film, young people!) on a tripod, set the timer, and take a picture of us posing on some Mickey-Mouse-head playground bars. After we took the picture, my new husband looked at me adoringly and spoke Spanish. This is every white girl's dream, right? Tall, dark, handsome, Latin. So of course I should just bat my eyelashes to whatever he says. Nope. Not me. I need to correct his grammar because I *am* that person.

"*Tay Co no co*," he says to me.

"What?" I ask, scrunching my face as though someone just made me eat sashimi (a.k.a. bait).

"*TAY CO NO CO*," he says louder, like I'm deaf rather than confused by his obviously messed-up pronunciation.

"What does that even mean?" I say, a lot less than lovingly, while jumping down from Mickey's ear.

"I know you," he says.

"Um, no. That's *Te conozco*. You chopped it up like the French Canadians do with French." We had a lot of French-Canadian visitors in South Florida, so I knew what I was talking about.

My new husband looked a little annoyed and a tiny bit unsure about the whole marriage to a grammar Nazi thing. He walked away from the giant metal mouse head and collected his camera and tripod.

A little less than three years after our honeymoon, we had our little rock star, the apple of my eye, our son. He is truly the best thing to come out of our starter marriage. That boy is going to be a rock star someday, and when he is, he owes me a Mercedes. Anyway, way before he picked up his first guitar and MacBook, we took our three-month-old rock star to his cousin's christening party. As soon as I saw the guest-of-honor baby, my jaw dropped. This poor little girl would obviously be asking Santa for a lifetime gift card to the laser hair removal place. The baby looked like a monkey. I'm not trying to be mean. I think monkeys are adorable, when they are actually monkeys. This human baby had dark hair everywhere. I mean, I didn't check the diaper region, but everywhere else was covered in dark hair. Good gosh. I was quiet for the afternoon in order to avoid accidentally announcing to everyone that the child could be an understudy for Cheeta on *Tarzan*. I held that in until we got in the car.

As soon as the doors were closed, I hit the husband with, "Your cousin's baby looks like a monkey."

"What? Lisa, you are so mean!" the husband yelled while maneuvering the car out of a cute Miami subdivision.

"It's true. Why do we have to pretend all babies are cute? Most of them look like old people. This one just happens to look like a monkey." I totally wasn't getting why this was offensive. It was true.

"You're such a bitch." he said to me, shaking his head and turning up the radio.

I wanted to hit him, but he was driving and that kind of distraction could lead to an accident. I didn't bother to reply. *What was the point?* He was getting all touchy about me calling 'em like I see 'em. That kid looked like a monkey. She is seventeen now, and every so often, I still wonder if she has found laser hair removal or at least wax along the way. I hope she found a date to the prom.

Back at the homestead, our misunderstandings grew, and we eventually grew apart. So when our son was three, we separated for good. Now that I'm not married to him, I think my ex-husband is pretty cool. He probably still thinks I'm a bitch. Whatever.

LISA R. PETTY SPECIALIZES IN BRUTALLY HONEST, SELF-DEPRECATing humor. She's a three-cat, crazy writer who also happens to have two dogs—which means she spends a lot of time talking to animals. They haven't started talking back. Yet. She began writing when she was seven, when she would jot down alternate plot lines for the Saturday-morning cartoons. *Misfit Academy* is her first published novel. She is currently writing *The Lizard King Club*, a novel that explores what would happen if certain members of the 27 Club reincarnated. She also likes to blog, eat her husband's delicious cooking, embarrass her teen son, and spend way too much time on Facebook and Twitter.

Dog Days of Moving

By Stacey Gustafson

ALL I NEEDED TO KNOW ABOUT MOVING I LEARNED from having a baby: there will be crying, shit happens, and you will swear never to do it again.

After my husband and I moved for the fourth time in five years of marriage, I could pack up a house before he came home for dinner. Box up kitchen supplies, check. Bubble wrap fragile items, no problem. Shut down utilities, piece of cake. But this time we had a fourteen-pound hitch to our smooth plans: our three-month-old baby girl who presented a new set of issues. What will I do when my baby needs a nap? Where will I breastfeed? How can I stay out of the movers' way? I needed an escape plan for the next twelve hours.

"It's settled," said my husband, Mike, plopping down in the nearest recliner. "I'll organize the move at the old house, and you stay at Jim and Mary's new home." Our friends lived nearby, and had no kids. They'd be at work, and I could hang out at their place. It was the perfect layover spot.

On packing day, a team of burly men wearing weight-lifting belts tackled our belongings in a flurry of plastic wrap, packing paper, and clear tape. This was my cue to dodge the chaos. Armed with extra diapers, wet wipes, a car seat, a bouncy seat, blankets, and baby toys, I held Ashley over my shoulder and banged on Jim and Mary's front door at 6:00 a.m.

"Gosh, thanks for letting us stay here," I said, rocking in place. "It's a mess at our house."

"Glad to help," Jim said. "Mary usually works from home, but today she's out of town. Do you mind letting Max out later?" Max, their golden retriever, danced around at the mention of his name.

"Got it," I said with a smile. "See you after work."

I spread a soft blanket on the living room floor and set up the rest of the baby gear. I sang to Ashley as I carried her around and pointed out all the new sights, like fresh flowers on the end table and a fuzzy dog toy. She jumped whenever Max barked.

"It's okay," I said to Ashley. "He's friendly." The dog licked her tiny arms with his wet tongue.

After I breastfed, she rubbed her eyes with her pudgy fists, which signaled naptime. I put her into the car seat on the coffee table, grabbed a *People* magazine, and snuggled on the sofa.

Max tap-danced near the back door, toenails clicking on the tile floor.

I'm coming, I'm coming.

He bolted outside and scrambled behind a tree. I snooped around their backyard. *Nice place.* Jim must be doing well at his sales job.

Max finished his business and scratched at the screen door to get back inside. I turned the doorknob and—*locked?* I twisted the knob faster than a DJ at a rave party. It wouldn't budge.

My mind whirled with a million bad things that could happen in the next few minutes. My baby might crash down off the coffee table. My chest heaved. My heart raced. What if she chokes, and I can't help her? Or someone steals her when I'm not looking?

I dashed to the front of the house and cut my legs on the rose bushes in my way. I spied my precious bundle through the window, tucked in a car seat, smack dab in the center of the coffee table. Asleep.

I'm going to kill Mike. This is all his fault. I never wanted to move in the first place.

Back in the day, cell phones were only used by corporate hotshots, not stay-at-home moms. I banged on the neighbor's door.

"I locked my baby in Jim's house and can't get back in," I screeched, twisting my wedding ring. "Can I use your phone?"

CLASH OF THE COUPLES

"Oh dear," the neighbor lady said waving me into the kitchen.

First, I called Mike. "Help," I whined. "Jim's back door automatically locked behind me. Ashley's trapped inside."

"I can't leave. I'm stuck here with the movers," he said. "Call Jim. He's got the key."

A meltdown brewed deep in my gut. My eyes twitched, and my arms flushed a deep crimson.

Did this man not understand what I was saying? Call the police or SWAT team for god's sake. Do something!

"DID-YOU-HEAR–ME-COR-RECT-LY?" I said. "ASH-LEY'S-LOCKED-IN-SIDE-THE-HOUSE-IN-A-CAR-SEAT-YOU-IDIOT. GET-HERE-NOW!"

"She'll be okay for a few minutes," he said with a sigh. "Just call Jim."

"You're such a jerk. You only care about yourself. I can't believe we've moving again."

I slammed down the phone and called Jim. "Ashley's locked inside your house. I need you to come home now."

"Uh ... I can leave in about an hour and a half."

"If you're not here in fifteen minutes, I'm breaking down the door," I shouted.

"I'm leaving."

I darted around the house again and checked for open windows or unlocked doors. Their place was sealed as tight as the packaging on a stack of baseball cards.

Someone tapped my shoulder.

"Need help?" asked a lanky, dark-haired, older guy. "I live next door."

"I'm so happy to see you. I'm staying at Jim and Mary's. I can't get back in the damn door, and my baby's inside."

He used a screwdriver to shake the sliding glass door off its rails. Like a genie, he lifted the glass door and, POOF, we were inside.

I ran to the living room, snatched up Ashley, and held her tight. She cried out in surprise.

"Thanks so much," I said to the neighbor with a big hug. "I was freaking out. You're my savior."

Out front, two cars screeched to a halt. I rushed outside with Ashley in my arms, Max following close behind.

"Honey, are you okay?" my husband asked and then planted a smooch. "I'm so sorry."

"God, I'm glad to see you. I can't wait until we get to our new place. I love you."

"Thanks for helping," Jim said to his neighbor, shaking his hand. "I got out of work as fast as I could."

"It turned out fine," I said. "Hey, there goes Max."

I stared as Max raced down the street and rounded the corner at the end of the road. Jim took off for the chase.

"See you in an hour and a half," I yelled after Jim as Mike and I strolled to the car.

STACEY GUSTAFSON IS AN AUTHOR, HUMOR COLUMNIST, AND blogger who has experienced the horrors of being trapped inside a pair of SPANX. Her blog, Are You Kidding Me?, is based on her suburban family and everyday life. Her short stories have appeared in Chicken Soup for the Soul and seven books in the Not Your Mother's Book series. Her work appears in Midlife Boulevard, Erma Bombeck Writers' Workshop, ZestNow, More Magazine, Pleasanton Patch, Lost in Suburbia, Better After 50, and on her daughter's bulletin board. She lives in California with her husband and two teenagers who provide an endless supply of inspiration. She writes about parenting and daily frustrations like her dislike of the laundry, self-checkout lanes, public restrooms, Brussels sprouts, roundabouts, and being middle-aged. Her book, Are You Kidding Me? My Life With an Extremely Loud Family, Bathroom Calamities, and Crazy Relatives, was published in 2014.

The Engagement that Almost Wasn't

By Meredith Napolitano

M Y HUSBAND AND I DON'T REALLY FIGHT. EVER.
Now before you get all Dr. Phil on me and let me know that fighting can be a *healthy* part of a relationship and that this is strange behavior and that we should be worried, you need to understand that this doesn't mean we never get annoyed with each other or disagree. We do that a *very* healthy amount. We make snippy comments and debate whatever issue it is. But we typically resolve our disagreements with no hurt feelings or lingering resentments. When it comes to knock-down, drag-out fights, we don't really have them.

Until we do.

And when they happen—they're monumental.

Thinking back to what was probably our most "ambitious" argument, it's a wonder that we ever it made it to husband and wife. Because *this* fight almost derailed our engagement.

About six months before we officially got engaged, my husband left his job. He'd been working for a startup that had excellent promise initially, but was riddled with bad luck that left a dark cloud hovering over the office. He was frustrated by the long hours, the on-the-cheap travel on virtually no notice (driving to the Canadian border to share a hotel room on the wrong side of the tracks), and the constant frustration. He had been miserable, and I totally supported his decision to quit.

Before he made the decision to leave, we'd been talking about marriage and our future together, and we continued talking about it afterwards. But we knew that until he had some type of steady income, a diamond was probably not the smartest way to spend the rest of his savings. He was lucky that he *had* some savings, along with virtually no debt and a place to live, but we knew that would eventually run out. He needed another job.

During these talks, we'd been browsing wedding sites together, and even picked a tentative date. For all intents and purposes, we *were* engaged, just without an official proposal or ring. When a new job was finally secured and our future seemed clear, my excitement started to build. But of course, he had some catching up to do. I wasn't expecting a ring the day he signed the new contract.

With the new job, he stayed at his parent's house during the week, and on Fridays he'd drive to my apartment and spend the weekend with me. We'd frequently email and call each other, but on busy weeks, there *would* be lapses in communication. That's why we always looked forward to Friday afternoons.

One particular Thursday, I was browsing wedding sites before work, and I found a funny article on the homepage about groom mishaps and bloopers: what not to wear, what not to say, what not to do on your most special day. I was laughing at the stories of toasts gone wrong and pants put on backwards. I knew he'd get a kick out of it, too, so I copied the link, pasted it into an email, and went off on my merry way to work.

We never talked on Thursday nights (I worked my second job and usually didn't have time to go home in between), so I didn't think anything of his radio silence. He'd just started a new job, so random emails might not have been in the cards. I did think it was weird that he hadn't responded at all to the stories, though, so I sent a follow-up email:

"Okay, so which one do you see yourself emulating?"

No response.

Weird.

On Friday, I left school and called him.

Me: "Hey stranger! What time are you planning to get here?"

Him: "Oh, am I still allowed to decide if I come?"

Me: "Uhhh ... sure, I guess."

Him: "So I can make some decisions on my own?"

Me: "Okay. I guess I was just wondering. I sort of thought you'd be here."

Him: "Fine. I'll leave now. And then we'll figure out if I should plan on coming back."

We hung up, and I started freaking out. What the *HELL?* What happened? Why was he so *cold?* I mean, seriously, we'd been joking about over-the-top weddings only a few days ago on the phone, and now he was saying he didn't want to come *back?* Who does that? I spent the next thirty minutes bouncing between fear and anger and nursing a horrible pit in my stomach. I couldn't even sit down.

He arrived and, making sure I saw him, balled up a little yellow piece of paper and threw it at me.

Him: "You want it that bad? It's yours."

Me: "What?"

Ignoring the yellow weapon of mass destruction he'd hurled, we started arguing. About how he thought I was turning into a control freak. About how he'd run so hot and cold that I didn't know if I could take it. About how my true feelings had come out once I knew he'd be making money again, and I could get something out of it. About how he was blindsiding me with doubts.

We yelled. We accused. I cried.

Finally, he told me that the link I'd sent him had been the last straw. He told me to pick up the paper and see how he was *dragging his feet.*

It was an odd thing to say, but since we could both use the breather before I ordered him out of my apartment, I picked it up, if for no other reason than to stall.

It was a layaway receipt from a jeweler.

WHAT?

Him: "You think I need ideas? You think I need a plan? *There's* your plan."

Me: "What?"

Him: "I put a deposit down the *day* I signed my contract. Excuse me for not just cleaning out my entire account and driving right down here."

Me: "*What?*"

Him: "To read that article was an insult to everything about me."

Me: "Wait, *what?*"

Him: "The article you sent me."

Me: "What article? The wedding blooper one?"

Him: "NO, the how to propose one."

Me: "We're not having the same argument, are we?"

We pulled up his email (back in the days of dial-up, so you know we were committed to the truth). I clicked the link in the email I'd sent, and we were transported to the wedding website—to some random article about gowns.

Me: "This isn't the one I sent to you."

Him: "No, it's not."

Me: "I sent you one about wedding bloopers."

Him: "No, you sent me one about how to propose."

And the light went on.

The link I'd sent him was for the homepage of the site, not any article in particular. When I was on the site, the main article was the funny bloopers. I managed to find it, and we read it together. He had pretty clearly never seen it before. By the time he had clicked, the homepage had changed, and the lead article was titled:

Are you ready?

Are you cringing?

Here it comes—

Dragging His Feet? How to Give Him the Hints He Needs for the Proposal of Your Dreams!

The article was full of subtle hints, sneaky ways to let him know what rings you like, romantic set-ups to give him the perfect backdrop, and so on. It even suggested some sample scripts that you could point out to his best guy friend so he would know exactly what to say.

As far as he was concerned, I had sent him an email telling him to *quit dragging his feet* and with an actual script of how I'd like to be proposed to.

A SCRIPT!

So this guy, who had been feeling down on his luck for months trying to find a job, after agonizing over his decision to leave his first job, who had feelings of guilt over his inability to move us forward, thought that I was—

I could not even wrap my head around what he must've been thinking. Frankly, I'm surprised he came over at all.

The yelling, the throwing, the betrayal, the insults, the worst throw-down, knock-out, one-of-us-isn't-coming-out-of-this-alive uproar—we were having two completely different arguments. Over a one-line link in an email. Thankfully, our story has a happy ending. He felt bad for spoiling the surprise. I felt bad for starting the whole thing. We had a lovely weekend and decided to stop talking about wedding stuff at all until we actually had a ring on my finger and a date on the calendar.

And in two weeks, we did.

Now, as an old married couple who just celebrated our tenth anniversary, we still remember our three rules of fighting.

1) When instigating a fight, state *exactly* why you are mad.

2) No throwing things.

3) And, most importantly of all, always, always, always check any link you send in an email. Twice.

Maybe even three times.

MEREDITH NAPOLITANO OF FROM MEREDITH TO MOMMY IS A former music teacher and choir director who made the move to stay-at-home mom two years ago. Meredith began writing shortly after this transition, initially as a way to continue having adult conversation without bombarding her friends constantly with daily anecdotes. Since her beginning, Meredith has slowly moved into the freelance writing and blogging world. She shares daily anecdotes of two little girls and a work-at-home husband, as well as reflections about parenting, silly stories, and moments that become memories. Most of all, she writes about the balance between her two roles of "Meredith" and "Mommy." Her writing has been featured on many different sites including The Huffington Post, Scary Mommy, Circle of Moms, and iVillage. Meredith was recently in the anthologies *I Just Want to Be Alone, My Other Ex,* and *Motherhood: May Cause Drowsiness.* When she's not fulfilling her role as chauffeur, housekeeper, cook, boo-boo kisser, and teacher, she's connecting with other moms on social media.

Hair of the Dog? Nope, It's Mine.

By Chris Dean

I GREW UP IN THE MIDWEST, WHERE YOUNG LADIES ARE taught the proper etiquette of disagreement from an early age. Unlike the less-evolved males on the playground, we do not push, punch, kick, or even yell. Oh no! Ours is a much more civilized form of warfare. We go straight for the emotional jugular vein, using our sweet words as cannon balls to blow a hole in your soul. *The victor?* The chick who gets her way.

Even though I discovered early on that I excelled at this form of emotional kung fu, I much preferred to keep the company of guys. Not only were you able to see their attacks coming, but they were totally blind to the female art of war. For me, it was a total win-win. At least it was until I met my husband.

The Hubs and I had worked together at a restaurant for a couple of years before we decided to give dating a go. As friends, I'd watched him go through a string of nasty relationships, and he'd watched my first marriage implode.

To everyone around us, we were totally wrong for each other, but from our point of view, life had simply gotten us to where we needed to be to find one another. We just made sense—right up until our first big fight and my meltdown, which left me trying to explain the inexplicable for months afterwards.

It was a Thursday afternoon, and we were finishing up our shifts with plans to eat some dinner, watch a little TV, and fall asleep on the couch together. Then some jackass had to go and call off for the night shift. My husband caught me on my way out the door to tell me he might have to stay if he couldn't find someone to cover the sick guy's position.

And I lost my shit.

I didn't lose it like a tantrumming toddler (yet). It was the far deadlier, internal snap that occurred. You know, the one that involves an outwardly pleasant yet stiff smile with a slight eye twitch, alerting the more observant person to the Stupid Storm going on inside your head? Yeah, that.

All the way home, I fumed. I mean, we had plans! That's—sacred! Or at least, it should be. Being young(ish) and in love automatically trump being all responsible and willing to cover some stupid shift in the kitchen, right? Hell yeah, they did!

At least in *my mind* it all made sense.

Part of my fury was undoubtedly due to the fact that my ex had been a work-a-holic who, during the last couple years of our marriage, had refused to even acknowledge that there was a difference between "place of employment" and "home." And here I was, in yet another relationship where work was becoming more important than me—at least, that was what my internal voice was screaming.

Well not *this* time, buster! I wanted my take-out and night of watching WWE and by golly, I was going have my night of take-out and watching WWE!

I slid into the driveway like I was in a NASCAR race on a dirt track, hit the front door like a ton of bricks, and dove for the phone, dialing at the speed of pissed. As soon as the poor guy answered, I informed him "we" were not going to work. Because that's the best way to get your way, right? Emotional blackmail?

I cut his confused *"What the hell, Chris?"* off at the knees, yelling that I couldn't be with a man who felt work was more important than I was. Then I did the ultimate chick move and hung up on him.

I literally checked my watch as I grabbed a beer from the fridge and began the countdown. It'd take him five minutes to clock out and run to his truck. It would take another thirty minutes, with traffic, to reach my house. That's when he'd burst through the door, proclaiming his undying love and begging me to give him another chance to prove that nothing in this world came before me!

So I sat down and waited. And waited. And waited some more.

At the forty-five minute mark, I began pacing. Was traffic bad? Did he stop to buy me flowers? Oh, he'd better have. And chocolates too.

At the hour point, I called the restaurant to make sure he'd understood that we'd just broken up. I mean, he was a guy, so maybe the subtlety of the situation had been lost on him.

He'd left the restaurant alright. Granted, it was ten minutes after our call and not five, but he'd left and, according to my source, he'd even been in a good mood. A GOOD MOOD? That was when the can of beer in my hand miraculously morphed into a bottle of tequila, because I needed some clarity of mind to puzzle this shit out.

Seeing as how I'm a chick and, as such, have developed an extensive network of completely partial sources, I was able to track the man's whereabouts to a club of the more *gentlemanly* variety, drinking beer with his friends. *Apparently*, they were all laughing and enjoying a laid-back evening together, doing whatever it is guys do at those spots.

It took another three phone calls, confirming the intel from the first, for the whole "laughing and having a fine time" thing to fully sink in. Where were the tears and heartbreak? Where was the wallowing in misery at having lost the best woman ever to walk into his life? Where, I ask, were my flowers and chocolate?

I remember things like rage, hurt, confusion, more rage, and tequila flowing freely that night. After that, everything went all fuzzy until I woke up the next morning, each tooth wearing its own wool sock, each apparently made out of the hair of a wet, unwashed dog. (My tongue was wearing the matching sweater.)

In case you've been lucky (and sensible) enough never to have gone on a tequila bender, the first thing to run through your mind after a quick assessment of your teeth's unfortunate morning apparel is: "WHY?" Possibly followed by, "Just let me DIE!"

Then it starts to sink in that, somewhere behind your eyes, evil trolls are playing very loud jungle drums. All of that would be bad enough without your stomach suddenly catching boogie fever and deciding to dance along to the beat. At that point, the only thing you're thinking is, "Can I make it to the bathroom before Jose Cuervo comes back for a morning visit?"

And that was where my fun really began.

Carefully, oh so carefully, I rolled out of bed and began the tip-toe of shame down the hall to the bathroom. I was gazing intently at the floor in an effort to avoid the daylight (eye-daggers made of retina-searing sunbeams) when I realized there was a trail of what looked like hair leading toward my bathroom.

But it wasn't any old hair, it was hair dyed my signature color of red: #66 Ruby Fusion. And there appeared to be a *lot* of it!

Since one hand was holding onto the wall and the other was clamped over my mouth to keep Mr. Cuervo in his rightful place, I couldn't reach up to check my mop that, suspiciously, was not hanging in my eyes this morning. This was when my simple prayers changed from, "Just let me make it to the john," to, "Oh, please let that hair not be mine!" A complete stranger's hair trailing down the hall to my bathroom was apparently a far better option than it being my own.

I paused at the door just long enough to take in the clippers sitting on the sink and the hair that was—EVERY-WHERE! It was like a clown wig had exploded all over my Room of Requirement while I'd slept! There was simply no way it could be my hair because I didn't even have that much hair on my whole friggin' head.

After giving up the ghost and releasing Jose back into the wilds of the porcelain throne (because I could only handle one crisis at a time on my best of days), I took a deep breath and looked in the mirror.

Somehow, in my tequila-fueled evening of heartbreak, shaving my head must have made some kind of sense. Because that is exactly what I'd done the previous night. A quarter-inch of unnaturally red fuzz was all I had left, except for a fine fringe of bangs. Apparently, even in my quasi-blackout state, I remembered I couldn't pull off a haircut that didn't include bangs to hide my massive forehead.

I tried playing the "look on the bright side" game. I was going save a ton of money on styling products and cut half an hour off the time it took me to get ready for work, which was awesome, since I was going need that time to guzzle coffee, curse tequila, and pray for death.

Obviously, the Hubs and I had a long talk (after we both stopped being hungover) and came to an agreement. For his part, he agreed he was a grown-ass man who wanted to be with a grown-ass woman and not someone who played high school games. I agreed I'd never again use emotional kung fu to try to get my way.

Over the years, we've always kept to that early-on agreement. We talk through the things that get under our skin (even if that talk occasionally follows a loud disagreement), we love and respect the other person enough not to fall back on old patterns of emotional blackmail, and we never play, as he so eloquently put it, "high school games."

As for those long-ago days following the meltdown? That man proved beyond a shadow of a doubt that he did indeed love me and placed me above all other things in his life (including a little bit of his pride) without needing to say a single word. After all, he held my hand, took me out to dinner, and was willingly seen with me in public the entire time my hair was way-too-slowly growing back.

And he hasn't let me forget about it to this day.

CHRIS DEAN WRITES AT PIXIE.C.D. (FORMERLY LIFE YOUR WAY!) where she shares acts of stupidity, life with adult offspring, and the occasional useful bit of info on life with chronic illness. She lives in Indiana with her amazingly tolerant hubby (who swears he doesn't mind putting up with her), their four adult kids, and a petting zoo of cats, dogs, chickens, Muscovy ducks, and geese she's systematically turned their home and yard into. When not writing, you can find her avoiding laundry and on her favorite social media sites.

Food Fight

By Linda Roy

THEY SAY FOOD IS LIFE. I CAN VOUCH FOR THAT SENTIment, because my husband and I fought over the subject for a good chunk of the early days of our relationship. I'm talking about completely ridiculous, heated debates over where, how, what, and even why we would consume something at any given time.

When two people decide to live together in any capacity, it brings with it the very heady consideration of merging two often differing food opinions. If you're a couple, either living together or entering into the holy bonds of matrimony, there's a lot riding on it. Chances are his mama's cooking is forever and lovingly lodged in the deepest recesses of his cranium and his stomach, crossing over and heading straight for the heart, while you're probably mimicking everything your mother did throughout your childhood. Sometimes it works out. And sometimes, never the twain shall meet.

My husband's mother was a native of Cleveland just like me, so we both came from a very meat-and-potatoes sensibility. The standard fare from both of our 1970s youths consisted of stews, pot roasts, mashed potatoes, spaghetti, Sloppy Joes, grilled cheese—you get the idea. But this is where things veer off into somewhat uncharted territory. My mother made her mashed potatoes from scratch, while his mother made hers from a box. But from there on, it all flip-flopped.

Did my mother ever venture into fish curry territory? No. Did she ever make beef bourguignon, for crying out loud? Nope. Am I saying my mother was a lousy cook? No way. Her mother didn't cook much at all, so she learned quite a bit on her own, and I remember the majority of what was presented at our kitchen table during my childhood fondly.

Our mothers both came from the Betty Crocker age of convenience, so who could blame my mother for making a casserole that consisted of tuna fish and noodles covered in crushed potato chips and announcing that we were having fish and chips? Okay, I blamed her. I *still* blame her for that. I guess what I'm saying is that my husband is a little more used to the adventurous approach, and, despite the ubiquitous Hungry Jack mashed potatoes, perhaps they had a more wholesome approach to dining. Nowadays, I think you'd call it organic, locally sourced, or hand-tossed as opposed to boxed and "incorporated" by a KitchenAid hand mixer.

Thinking about the early days of grocery shopping duality with my betrothed is an exercise in PTSD, slight humiliation, utter rage, and complete hilarity. We're both stubborn people, and you might say we were consumed with our preconceptions regarding consumption. We'd both been on our own for a number of years. He knew how to cook and so did I. But while he was a little more driven toward his dog-eared encyclopedia of food, I was all about convenience. I was a boil-in-a-bag girl. If you can reconstitute it, you can whip it up and be eating it in no time flat, leaving more time for things like sex. And who's the wiser?

Turns out he was.

When I lunged for the boxed scalloped potatoes, he'd yank the box from my hands, righteously spouting off ingredients like a battle rapper at a poetry slam. "Dextrose, mono sodium glutamate, dried potato 'product,' powdered cheese—"

"Yeah, so what's wrong with that?" I'd protest.

"What's wrong with that is that none of it is natural. See the spices in this? Where it says 'spice blend'? You could put your own spices in here, use real potatoes, béchamel, and you'd have something way better than this. And it's cheaper."

Blah blah blah. All I heard was what I perceived as his snooty self-righteousness, when actually, as I would later admit—much later—it was his *rightness*.

He went on to pontificate further, "My roommate in college studied advertising. He'd come home all the time and tell me about how companies use the cheapest ingredients and sell them at two or three times the actual cost, advertising them as convenience foods."

"What's wrong with convenience?" I wanted to know.

"Nothing, except you're paying too much, and it tastes like crap."

Crap? I was quick to point out right there in aisle seven of the Stop & Shop that I liked my convenience. I liked my mono sodium glutamate, the flavor of which was unparalleled. Give me *more* salt. In fact, lace it with Morton's, and shut the hell up!

That's when it happened. Right there, in front of God, all of aisle seven, and overflowing audibly into every other aisle for that matter, it was a full-on call for "attention all shoppers!" My behavior miraculously became synonymous with my aisle number as I stomped my feet, bashed the cart into the shelves, caused an avalanche of Potato Buds ("Clean up in aisle seven"), and it didn't stop there.

"You can't tell me I can't have what I want! Who's going to peel and slice all of those potatoes, huh? Who's going to make *béchamel?* You want me to put, what ... nutmeg in that? My mother had the same container of dried parsley in the cupboard for fifteen years. I didn't grow up in the friggin' McCormick's factory, mister!"

"Whoa, whoa! Relax! We're just talking about potatoes here."

Telling me to relax was his first mistake. Never, ever tell a woman to relax. That just gets us going. That builds the proverbial steam in the pressure cooker. See? I *do* know how to cook. And we were most certainly not talking about potatoes anymore. We were talking about control. Was I staring down the barrel of forsaking all that I had grown accustomed to, rolling up in the fetal position, readying myself for a lifetime of arrogant lectures about everything from food preparation to the way things worked in the world? I'd been places, done things; just let me have my goddamned reconstituted potatoes! Of all the things he chose to take a stand on, did this Hungry Jack poster child of the 1970s have to mess with my Betty Crocker scalloped-potato sensibilities?

And then it dawned on me. Maybe that's why he's taking a stand. Maybe after years of reconstitution, he'd decided to draft a new constitution and that meant real food. And after all, didn't I want to do nice things for my guy? Didn't I want to make the effort? Were dried-up potatoes really worth all that fuss?

Yes, and yes, but also yes!

"You've always gotta have it your way!" I whined. "Well it's not just about how you grew up. It's about how I grew up too!"

"How were the vegetables?" he asked.

Well, that just wasn't playing fair. Nothing needed to be said. He knew. He knew they were a drab, sickly green. He knew they came oozing out of a can covered in their own sodium-enriched glop sauce, and were then overcooked in a pan probably containing dangerous levels of aluminum, which only enhanced their flavor.

"Um ... yeah ... they sucked," came my reply.

"Of course they sucked."

God, I hate when he's right.

We cleaned up aisle seven while so many eyeballs trailed our every move it seemed like the final scene of *Officer and a Gentleman*, only in slow motion. But instead of clapping and shouting, "Way to go!" as I was swept away Debra Winger style, chest heaving with pride, they just muttered under their breaths. I was whisked away promptly, clutching an eight-pound sack of russet potatoes tightly to my breast.

Over the ensuing months and years, we learned to meet each other somewhere in the middle between béchamel and what the hell. After we were married, we went to his parents' house for Thanksgiving. His mother made the best Thanksgiving dinner I'd ever had. (Sorry, Mom.) Everything was delicious, and the potatoes were real. The stuffing was especially better than any I'd ever tasted. As I complimented my mother-in-law on the delicious meal, with particular emphasis on the stuffing, the entire table erupted with laughter.

"Oh thank you," his mother beamed, adding, "I wasn't going to make *that* mistake again."

"What mistake was that?" That's when they told me about the great Stove Top Stuffing Debacle of 1980.

"He was incensed. He was having none of it. He let me know that he'd come all the way from college for what amounted to seat-cushion filler, and he made such a stink about it, I decided it would be homemade from then on," his mother joked.

"But what *is* stuffing?" my husband asserted, evoking Socrates, or Sartre, or Jaques Pepin. He continued philosophically, "It's just some bread, milk, an egg, throw in a little celery, marjoram. It's *Thanksgiving* for god's sake! Why would you use *boxed* stuffing?"

He said it like she had assembled a meal of bird droppings and Ritz Crackers with more than a hint of betrayal in his petulant voice. That's when I saw his inner seven-year-old stomp his foot and declare enough!

His mother and I exchanged knowing looks. And while the whole thing is laughable today, and it sure seems stupid, it spoke volumes about what we become familiar with, what we'll compromise about, and basically begged the question: *How much are you willing to swallow your pride, along with the nutmeg-sprinkled béchamel and the occasional reconstituted potatoes?*

I knew it was all going to be okay. We'd weather the storm. It was only food, after all. He was right when he said that back there in aisle seven. It's just food. We eat to live, not live to eat. Maybe instead of loving to eat so much, we should eat to love? I don't know. Maybe that's too philosophical. It doesn't really have to mean anything. So Betty Crocker was a crock. Now I can make béchamel like nobody's business. He did me a favor. He did our kids a favor.

I was reflecting on some of this newly gained knowledge when my husband's mother announced it was time for dessert.

"Homemade pumpkin pie, Mom?"

"No, I got Mrs. Smith's."

Holy shit!

And so it begins.

LINDA ROY IS A HUMORIST, WRITER, AND MUSICIAN LIVING IN New Jersey with her husband and two boys. Her blog, elleroy was here, is a mix of humor and music that she refers to as "funny with a soundtrack." She served as Managing Partner and Editor-in-Chief at the politics and pop culture website, Lefty Pop, and was named one of BlogHer's Voices of the Year for 2014. Her work has appeared on The Huffington Post, Scary Mommy, In the Powder Room, Aiming Low, Humor Outcasts, Funny Not Slutty, Erma Bombeck Writers' Workshop, Midlife Boulevard, Mamapedia, Sprocket Ink, The Weeklings, BonBon Break, and Earth Hertz Records. She is the female Larry David and will criticize your parallel parking to prove it. When she's not snarking and kvetching, she's fronting the Indie/Americana band Jehova Waitresses.

An Apple a Day

By Dave Lesser

M Y WIFE AND I RECENTLY GOT INTO A FIGHT ABOUT her favorite caramel apples. Oddly, it wasn't about whether or not all the candy coating on the fruit completely negates any health benefits. She freely admits they're not good for her, they're just damn good. They're made by some lady named Mrs. Prindable, and they're really friggin' expensive (although sometimes, you can get a decent deal on them on QVC). They are some mighty fine apples, but really not worth yelling about. Except when they are.

Recently, Allie *confessed* that she had bought a box. Or maybe two, but the second was for gifts.

"They make great gifts!" I laughed and told her it wasn't a problem. We are a one-income family and try to avoid spending money on frivolous items, but everyone has a vice. Hers are fancy apples.

I was not, however, expecting the issue to come back, spewing hot metaphorical caramel in my face. The QVC order was completely out of my mind when the kids and I picked Allie up from the train station. I was in a pretty good mood. It had been a fun day as a stay-at-home parent, and I was feeling downright jovial. We were joking about something else (after the impending brouhaha, it's impossible to remember what) when she mentioned the apples. Our five-year-old daughter asked why she had bought them.

Instead of saying, "because they're the world's best apples" or something about treating herself, she said, "because your father didn't get them for me."

Ha! I thought it was funny, so I responded with a joke of my own, asking what she did to deserve them.

Not funny. *Apparently.*

I was kidding, of course. My wife is amazing. She works her ass off at her job and is a phenomenal mother. But I really didn't think I said anything wrong. It was a joke! It was a joke in response to her joke. The problem was that she wasn't joking. There were a couple reasons my wife was displeased with my words and (in)actions.

The first was that she shouldn't have to do anything to deserve receiving something she loves, something that I know she loves. Prior to making the purchase herself, she even mentioned to me that a friend of hers saw that QVC was doing a Christmas in July (or some such cockamamie nonsense) sale on the apples and thought of her.

"Oh, that's sweet," is what I think I said. There is nothing *necessarily* wrong with that response. I didn't realize, at the time, it was a (way too subtle for me) hint that I should buy her the apples! It should be noted that my wife tunes in for a certain QVC show like it is an actual show, one with some dude named David, a big fella who gets enormous pleasure from eating the products he's hawking. I have to admit, he makes even the crappiest frozen dinner look really tasty. I thought she just wanted to watch him eat the apples. (Even with the QVC discount, those suckers are expensive. And we're not exactly rolling in caramel and chocolate chips over here.)

I should've been more sensitive. *What guy shouldn't?* I should think to get my wife gifts throughout the year, because she's on my mind, and I see something I know would make her smile. And I love her smile. Blah blah blah. I get it. I take our marriage for granted sometimes. We've been together a long time, and it's hard not to. But I know I have to realize what I have and work to keep it. If that means buying some overpriced (but kind of worth it, because they really are damn good!) apples, that's what I should do.

All that could be forgiven. Allie knows who she married. I'm sensitive and thoughtful in other ways. Besides, it's not like she always thinks about me. Yes, chances are far better that if the shoe were on the other foot, she would have gotten me the random gift. But I wouldn't have been mad at her if she didn't! Why was she so pissed off?

Oh right. Because I totally ignored her birthday.

Not the last one, the one before that. *Geez, talk about holding a grudge.* Okay, I'm an asshole. And this was the crux of the caramel-apple argument. That year, Allie had asked me to plan a little party for her, invite some friends, and make it happen. One of her jobs at work is as an event planner, and she takes that role with family functions as well. She wanted something special planned for her that she could just show up at and have a great time. I never even got started. Her friends are so dispersed, and I wasn't even sure who she was still close with. At first, her birthday was so far away, then I got injured and had to have surgery, and then there wasn't enough time. And all bullshit excuses. I choked.

But it gets worse.

I didn't even make a nice birthday dinner for her to apologize. I didn't have time to go to the grocery store that day. I went to the gym instead.

It gets worse.

I didn't even get her a cake. *Good lord, why is she with me?* I really am an asshole.

But, oh yes, it gets even worse.

Allie's birthday is just before Father's Day, which she spent weeks planning to make special. She recreated, on a small scale, the obstacle course races I love to run, complete with a banner she'd spent days decorating. It was unbelievably thoughtful.

But I wasn't thinking about any of that when we were in the car. I have a short memory and, for me, this stuff was all in the distant past. Two whole birthdays ago! For Allie, it was still fresh. In fact, the only thing that made it better, truly healed us, and made us laugh about the whole damn thing was after things had settled down, I asked her to remind me about the details of how badly I screwed that birthday up. Wow. Her eyes lit up at the prospect. She remembered the timeline down to the minute, and it gave her such glee in the retelling, in finally getting it off her chest. The more uncomfortable I got, the happier it made her and the more she started cracking up. She could barely get the words out. I love her smile, so I couldn't help but smile and laugh right along.

But, man, I am asshole! *Sorry honey. You really deserve those caramel apples.*

DAVE LESSER IS A FORMER ATTORNEY WHO MUCH PREFERS HIS JOB as a stay-at-home dad to two hilarious and adorable children. His amazing wife fully supports his love of obstacle course, road, and trail races. He is a regular contributor to *TIME* magazine online, The Huffington Post, and The Good Men Project, and he blogs at Amateur Idiot Professional Dad.

Neurotic in Lisbon

By Camille DeFer Thompson

I DON'T TRAVEL WELL. UNFAMILIAR SURROUNDINGS, local customs, and alternate forms of transportation all freak me out. So when my new husband suggested that we take a three-week trip to Portugal to visit his relatives, my head screamed *NO!* Sure, it would be exciting to visit this historic city in the springtime—quaint outdoor cafés, charming ancient castles, and blah blah blah. But it would also mean getting used to foreign food, foreign money, and even a foreign language, for Christ's sake.

"It'll be great, Hun," Jerry said, slipping his arm around my shoulder. "Just think ... all those cool European shops, crammed with ... uh ... handbags and shoes ... and ... handbags." Exploiting my weakness for fine leather goods? It was a hand well played.

After twelve hours in the air and another four in airport terminals, I couldn't wait to jump into a hot shower as soon as we arrived at our hotel. A little woozy with jet lag, I unpacked a few things and headed into the bathroom, armed with my travel-size bottles of shampoo and conditioner. I adjusted the water temperature and noticed a cord dangling against the back wall of the tub enclosure. *Hmmm, it must operate the shower curtain,* I thought. I stepped in the tub and gave the cord a little tug. An ear-piercing horn sounded, summoning my husband, three maids, and the hotel paramedics. I stood paralyzed, wide-eyed, and shivering in a stiff white bath towel.

Jerry explained, in his marginal Portuguese, that I had pulled the alarm cord by mistake, and assured everyone that I was perfectly fine. "So sorry, uh ... *sinto muito,*" he said, handing each of the attendants a coin. They nodded in appreciation and left, glancing over their shoulders at the drippy, blushing American woman.

"*Imbecil,*" I heard one of them mumble.

Once I recovered from my first encounter with culture shock, I was ready to tackle the city streets. However, it soon became obvious that in Lisbon, pedestrians are viewed as targets—they take their lives into their hands as they sprint across the narrow, busy streets, dodging speeding Alfa Romeos and Ferraris.

Thinking I could avoid bodily injury by merely following the rules of the road, I waited on the sidewalk for the green walk signal to light up and then stepped off the curb. A dusty Fiat whizzed past me, honking wildly, sending me with a clumsy leap back onto the sidewalk. Was he honking to signal his approach or merely to express his annoyance that I might have caused him significant delay had he actually hit me?

Once downtown, I marveled at the colorful shops displaying handmade pottery and linens, as well as the promised high-end leather merchandise. My husband had exchanged our traveler's checks at the local bank, and he doled out some bills to me. This was a few years back, so it was before Portugal adopted the Euro.

Strolling down the walking streets on which cars are prohibited, undoubtedly for the express purpose of prolonging the life span of tourists, I flashed my one-thousand-*escudo* notes at the merchants. *That'll earn me a little respect*, I thought.

"The rich American has arrived," they'll whisper, "to spend her wealth in our humble establishments."

"Thanks, sweetie," I said to my husband, fanning the bills out like a poker hand. "I've never seen this generous side of you. Mommy likes."

"Relax," he said. "They're only worth about seven bucks."

Next, we ventured to St. George's Castle, a picturesque structure perched atop one of Lisbon's hills, showcasing sculptures and lush gardens within ancient walls. I strolled along a stone path until the call of nature led me to a public restroom, where I queued up in a short line. A middle-aged matron directed patrons to stalls as they were vacated. After a few moments, it was my turn. Taking the opportunity to check my makeup while there, I had just begun to reapply my lipstick when the attendant started banging on the door, firing out Portuguese prose.

What the—

I fumbled frantically for the latch, wondering what manner of emergency could prompt such an attack on a restroom stall door. Flood, famine, plague? When I finally opened the door, I was greeted by the old lady who offered a smiling, *"Obrigada,"* (thank you) and handed me a paper towel. *Thank you? Uh, you're welcome?*

The bathroom calamities didn't stop there. I'd been warned by my frequent-flyer friends that, in European countries, toilet paper is sometimes in short supply. "Best to tuck a little into your pocket for emergencies," was the advice. Fearing that each roll I encountered might be my last, I appropriated a few sheets at every opportunity. Before long, I had wads of Euro-Charmin crammed in my coat crevices, overflowing my pants pockets, and trailing from my fanny pack. There was enough for six trips back to Lisbon.

By the end of week two, I'd had enough of cobblestone avenues, bumpy streetcar rides, and unrecognizable meal options. I craved a traditional American breakfast. We went to the restaurant next door to our hotel, and the waiter handed me a menu. By now, I knew a few Portuguese words. I pointed to the item with the word *"ovo"* in it. Eggs, that's what I wanted. Bacon and eggs with an English muffin. Was that too much to ask?

"Ah, *não, não*," he said, shaking his head and pointing to another selection.

"I just want eggs," I said, feeling my eyes fill with tears. I looked across the table at my husband. "Tell him. Tell him what I want."

He leaned toward me. "Honey," he said. "I don't think they have American-style eggs here. Maybe you better take his advice."

"Whatever!" I said, pounding the table with my fists. "Just bring anything," I screamed, mascara streaming down my face. Waving the waiter off, I slammed my arm into the water pitcher. He caught the vessel, righted it, and then slowly backed away from the table.

"I want to go home, dammit. I can't do this anymore. No one understands me, the money doesn't make sense, and if I see another fucking ancient ruin, I'll gouge my eyes out."

"Try to hold it together," Jerry said, nodding and smiling at the customers at adjacent tables. "It's only Thursday. We've still got another week here."

"Seriously?" I said, wiping my nose with the napkin. "That's all you've got? *Try to hold it together?* That's supposed to help?"

I was still distraught when our meals arrived.

I took a bite of the delicate white fish, one of the coastal city's culinary specialties. "This is so good," I said, sniffling. "Better than anything I've ever tasted, even in San Francisco." I sobbed through every delicious morsel.

The final week of our trip was drama free. In a shopping mall, Jerry found a McDonald's, and despite enduring cold burgers, limp fries, and soupy shakes, it served to satisfy my homeland craving. I even found a great deal on a trendy leather tote.

When our plane touched down at San Francisco International, I let out a long sigh. I couldn't wait to get to my favorite café to savor a buttery croissant and linger over a steaming latte. Now that's authentic Americana.

CAMILLE DEFER THOMPSON IS A FREELANCE WRITER AND blogger. Her short fiction and non-fiction is published in a number of collected works including *Written Across the Genres* and *Livermore Wine Country Literary Harvest*. Her humorous account of her near fatal attempt at DIY in "Jolt of Reality," appears in *Not Your Mother's Book ... On Home Improvement*. Her print feature articles appear in the Danville Times. Camille maintains a popular column, *Off Your Rocker*, on San Ramon Patch, which targets active seniors. She is also a regular contributor to Midlife Boulevard.

The Cake Heard Around the World

By Mary Widdicks

EVERY PERSON AND EVERY RELATIONSHIP HAS A BREAK-ing point: the proverbial straw that breaks the camel's Zen state and turns him or her into a raving lunatic. *I think that's how the story goes anyway.* I reached that point in my marriage two years ago when my husband bought his own birthday cake, after I'd spent all day making him one—and I nearly divorced him.

With time, and a considerable amount of self-reflection, I can now admit that my sweets-related meltdown might have been about more than just excess cake. I mean, with a cool head, one might point out that there can never be too much cake. However, at the time, that birthday cake represented every sock I'd ever found stuffed in weird places around the house, every time I'd sat down on the toilet only to be greeted by cold, wet pee droplets that I passive aggressively wiped off my posterior with my husband's towel, and every tissue that went through the laundry and would end up partially disintegrated and fused to my clothes. The cake incident was the tip of the iceberg and threatened to sink our already leaky ship.

It had been the most difficult period to date in our marriage. In the prior three months, my husband had started a new job and we'd moved internationally with our ten-month-old and two dogs, bought a new home, had the sale fall through on our old house, lived in an empty house for a month before our furniture arrived on the world's slowest boat, and weathered our first Midwest heat wave and drought. Adventures like these always sound romantic and exciting in theory or in retrospect, but in reality, they are just unpleasant.

They build character, right?

Maybe, but unfortunately they also build resentment and stress. After sleeping for a month on a fifty-dollar medieval torture device that Walmart had the nerve to call a futon, we were both looking for someone to blame for the pains in our butts, both figurative and literal. Looking back now, we refer to this time as "the dark days" because it felt like both of us were living in isolation, cut off from the outside world, even though we were living right beside each other. We were like prisoners living in neighboring cells.

We moved around each other like passive-aggressive zombies: responding only to stimuli, not really seeing each other. We rarely talked and fell into a habit of using badly interpreted gestures to give us a clue as to what the other person was thinking. We were both terrible at reading these clues.

Suddenly, every crumb he left on the counter was his way of telling me he was too busy to help out around the house, and every time I folded everyone's laundry but left his lying in a pile on his side of the futon from hell was my flipping him the bird in response.

Rather than asking for help, we were caught in a vicious cycle of trying to demonstrate to the other how busy we were by proving how little the other person did. Shockingly, it wasn't working, and we were slowly losing each other in a fog of anger and frustration.

Then my husband's birthday arrived. After months of freeze out, I was determined to make up for my poor showing as a wife by making him his favorite cake from scratch: red velvet. So I buckled my toddler into the back of our tiny, two-door hatchback and ventured out to the store. A frantic twenty minutes and two tantrums later, my son and I emerged victorious from the supermarket.

I put the baby down for his nap, resisted the urge to join him, and started baking. After discovering that red food coloring stains more than just food, I placed my hard-earned cake batter in the oven. I imagined how surprised my husband would be when he walked in from work just as I finished icing it. I had it all planned out.

Or so I thought.

What I didn't know was that my husband had set his own guilt-driven plans in motion. If at any point we had discussed our feelings and concerns about our relationship, the whole cake fiasco might have been avoided, but we didn't, and it wasn't.

In what probably seemed like a generous and maybe even romantic gesture to my husband at the time, he left work early that day and bought himself a birthday cake. *You know, to save me the trouble of making him one.*

When he walked through the door an hour early, proudly displaying his purchased cake like the spoils of a battle, suddenly the time for talking was past. I'm not sure if it was the fact that I'd spent all day making the cake, the fact that he didn't trust me to make him one, or the fact that despite how busy he claimed to be, he still managed to leave work early to undermine my wifely duties, but that cake became the root of all our problems.

I looked angrily from his clueless face to the offending baked good and back again. Slowly and calmly, like a tiger stalking her prey, I walked to the oven and removed the cake. It was still wobbly and uncooked, and when I slammed it on the counter, the red batter splashed everywhere. Without a word, I turned around and left the house.

I drove around for an hour, sobbing into the steering wheel over spilled cake, until finally I decided that irreconcilable birthday plans probably wasn't a good enough reason to divorce the father of my child. I turned the car around and slunk apologetically back to the house. That night we finally sat down and talked about how we'd both been feeling. As we scrubbed the floors and counters, trying to remove the red mess I'd made, we also attempted to wipe clean the last few months of our relationship. Sure, there are still a couple stains remaining on both as reminders of the great cake incident of 2011. Maybe they will always be there, but that night, as we scrubbed, we promised never to rely on crumbs, laundry, or cake to do our communicating for us. So I guess it wasn't a total loss. Plus, my husband learned never, under any circumstances, to buy his own birthday cake. *Ever.*

MARY WIDDICKS IS A MOM TO TWO BOYS AND TWO MALE DOGS. Once a cognitive psychologist, she now spends the majority of her time trying to outsmart her kids (and failing!). Currently, being the only female in the family means that sometimes her voice gets drowned out by fart jokes and belching contests. She started Outmanned so she'd have a place to escape the testosterone and share her hilarious life with the rest of the world. Mary's writing has been featured on parenting sites such as Mamapedia, Mamalode, In the Powder Room, and Scary Mommy. She is a regular contributor on BLUNTmoms, has been honored as a 2014 Voice of the Year by BlogHer, and was named Badass Blogger of the Year by The Indie Chicks.

The Cold War

By Courtney Conover

FRANKLY, I DON'T SEE THIS AS ONE SUCCINCT ARGUMENT so much as an ongoing disagreement about which the Hubs and I will never see eye to eye.

They say that there are three sides to every story: the two sides and the truth. But in this particular case, I am all but certain that there are indeed only two: mine—which, in fact, *is* the truth—and the Hub's, which by any objective standard, is a twisted tale comprised of lies and exaggerations of epic proportions.

It all boils down to what happened four years ago inside a hotel room on Florida's Hollywood Beach boardwalk. The irony is that the only things boiling within those four walls were our tempers. The problem was that the thermostat in the room had somehow been cranked dangerously low by someone—*cough, cough,* the Hubs—which he vehemently denies. Here's what really happened:

It was such a hot afternoon that hot water was coming out of both taps in the bathroom. After spending the entire morning lounging around the pool, the Hubs and I sought refuge in the comfort of our air-conditioned hotel room. Now, what happened next is a little murky. But what I can tell you definitively is that I went into the bathroom to take a shower, and when I came out, an icicle developed on my nose within two minutes.

It was abundantly clear that the Hubs had conveniently taken it upon himself to erroneously adjust the thermostat before he collapsed onto the bed, where he fell into a deep slumber. But get this: not before burying himself under the down comforter *first*. (In retrospect, he was already bracing for the polar vortex, but I digress.)

In an effort to keep my digits from developing frostbite, I set out to right the wrong by attempting to readjust the thermostat. But when I stood face to face with the thing, I had no idea how to operate the sucker. It seems that it would have been easier to figure out the formula for cold fusion. So I backed away and did the only thing I could to keep from freezing to death: I went outside on the patio. When I opened the sliding door, the initial blast of heat produced a veil of frost on both sides of the door. For a split second, I contemplated writing *Heat me!* with the tip of my index finger, but I decided against it.

After spending approximately fifteen minutes outside, my sweat was sweating. I waved the white flag and came crashing back inside the room.

"Jesus, Scott! *Really?* It's freezing in here!"

"Tell me about it." His muffled voice was barely audible underneath the covers.

"*Tell me about it?*" I mocked.

And that's when I came undone.

"I'll tell you about it, alright. Or better yet, why don't *you* tell me how you managed to withstand playing in a helmet and full pads in ninety-degree temps *for years*, but are now only able to sleep comfortably when it's thirty below."

Apparently, them's fightin' words.

"Oh, no you're not. You're not blaming this on me!" Scott blasted, as his head shot up from under the covers. "This coming from the woman who turns the ceiling fan on high ... in the wintertime ... when the heat's on! But do I say anything? *Nooo!* I just put up with it every ... single ... night!"

"Oh poor you! I must make it so uncomfortable!" I spat. I turned on my heel, started for the front door, and then promptly stubbed my toe on Scott's open suitcase, "... and how many times have I told you to move this effing thing?"

I grabbed my purse and fled to the lobby. I didn't know where I was going, but I knew I had to get the hell out of there. I felt angry, impulsive, and completely out of control, which, I had learned from previous experience, is a dangerous emotional cocktail. After buying a tabloid from the gift shop, I nursed my hurt feelings—and a gin and tonic—at the bar overlooking the beach.

So that, in a nutshell, is what happened.

But if you ask the Hubs, he somehow has an entirely different take. His version involves him being the innocent bystander in all of this. His version pens me as the aggressor. His version proclaims that he was just a tired hubby in need of a nap who awoke to find that he had been transplanted to Antarctica without leaving his hotel room:

"I don't really remember what happened. All I know is that I had a terrible headache when I returned from the pool and needed to lie down. Apparently, I fell asleep on top of the comforter, but was awakened by my inability to feel my toes. I mean, it was so cold in there, a polar bear would have cried for help. Thank goodness for down feathers. Otherwise, I don't know where I'd be today ..."

"I called out for Courtney to return the thermostat to its original setting, and when she didn't respond, I scanned the room and discovered she was nowhere to be found."

"I know she likes it on the cooler side. But to this day, I have no earthly idea why she'd do such a thing ..."

Yeah, okay.

After seven years of marriage, Scott and I continue to agree on many things—and when we don't, we make a point to discuss it.

But not this—not the cold war. This is futile.

What transpired inside that hotel room continues to be a sticking point with us. Like a bad penny, the issue of who messed with the thermostat that day keeps popping up over, and over, and over again, to no avail.

For example, the other night was unusually cold. I think if my memory serves, the low hovered somewhere around fifty degrees. Still, I stood idly by as Scott opened all three windows in our bedroom and turned the ceiling fan on. It was Hollywood, Florida all over again. And, of course, I couldn't help but point out that a pattern had been established here.

"I mean, really, Scott, how freakin' cold do you have to make it?" I said.

"*What?* You like it this way!"

Again, yeah, okay.

And this is why his woolen varsity football blanket holds court at the foot of our bed all year round.

COURTNEY CONOVER IS A MOM OF TWO AND THE WIFE OF FORMER NFL offensive lineman Scott Conover—and they will continue to bicker about the room temperature until death do them part. In the meantime, she has more Legos, hair products, and NFL memorabilia lying around her home than she knows what to do with. She is also a certified yoga instructor and a contributing writer to the *Chicken Soup for the Soul* book series. A graduate of the University of Michigan, Courtney was a television reporter and auto show model in her life BC (Before Children). When she's not blogging or obsessing over her hair (she wholeheartedly invites critics to flame away at her shallowness), she's cleaning up cold macaroni and cheese off the floor or tripping over Fisher-Price Little People. Her work has appeared on BlogHer, Scary Mommy, and USA Football. She blogs at The Brown Girl with Long Hair.

We're Political Opposites, and We're Not Above Yard-Sign Warfare

By Marie Bollman

YOU KNOW WHAT THEY SAY: IF YOU WANT TO STAY friends with someone, never talk about politics.

Well, I don't know who "they" are, but they've obviously never been married to their political polar opposite. When it comes to politics, my husband and I live in a house divided. I am a bleeding-heart Democrat who proudly volunteered for the Obama campaign in 2008. I'm as liberal as they come. He is a fiscal conservative who works in big business and wants small government. Although he's progressive on lots of social issues, he's a proud Republican. Long story short, we cancel each other out. Every single election, we are a complete and utter wash.

It didn't start out this way. We got married fourteen years ago when neither one of us was politically inclined. We were just kids with better things to worry about, but over the years, we've grown into our beliefs. And somehow, we've grown in opposite directions. Being a political odd couple hasn't been easy. In fact, there are times when it becomes a major stressor for us. Our political discussions have been known to become heated. It's gotten to the point where we can't watch political news coverage in the same room because we can't even agree on which channel to watch. There are times when I find myself wondering, "Who are you, and how did I end up married to you?"

Thankfully, we're not entirely dysfunctional. We've learned that we're doomed if we don't have a sense of humor about it all. We love ourselves some good old-fashioned political satire, especially *Saturday Night Live*. When the phone rings and it shows up as an unknown number, we actually race each other to the phone, just hoping it's a political survey so we can speak our political piece (in other words: give the opposing side a piece of our mind). For the record, I hold a very strong advantage in this department being that I am a stay-at-home mom and basically never get to leave the house. We are both constantly in a state of light-heartedly vying for our kids' political allegiance.

"Ben, promise me you won't grow up to be a Republican."

"Jack, when you get older, be one of the good guys. Conservatives are the smart ones."

"Come on, Anna, don't you want to make your mom proud and vote Democrat?"

It goes on and on. Our kids think it's funny.

Every four years when it's time for another presidential election, well that's when things in our house get really dicey. The first year we lived in our neighborhood, we laid it all out on our front yard for our lovely neighbors to see. It started when I bought my Obama yard sign and proudly dug those metal stakes into the ground, solid and firm. It was my declaration of Democratic devotion. My husband came home and said, "Well, that's not fair. You can't put that up. What will people think?"

"Of course I can. It's a free country. What are you going to do about it?" I asked defiantly.

My snarky comment was met with silence. Well, that sure shut him down. Bam!

I should've figured he was plotting passive-aggressive political warfare in that conservative mind of his.

Little did I know that later that day he went online and placed his order for his very own Romney yard sign. It showed up a week or so later. I actually watched him walk stoically down to the end of our driveway—look to the left at my Obama sign—look to the right at the empty patch of grass—and scornfully plant that reprehensible Republican sign directly across the driveway from mine.

Seriously? What the hell are the neighbors going to think? Oh my god, we are SO obnoxious!

In no time at all, we had neighbors stopping their cars in front of our house, rolling down their windows, and teasing us for our display of contention. We hardly knew these people and here they were making fun of us! We totally deserved it. But it wasn't embarrassing enough to make either of us back down. There stood our lawn signs, firmly planted in the ground like battle flags, just waiting for election night to determine a winner.

Yes, there were times when the weather came through and knocked both of our signs over. Of course, like any self-respecting wife, I put my own back up with great care. And maybe I just didn't notice his sign sitting over there in that sad little pile. Let's not forget the times when he would take out both signs so he could mow the lawn. Somehow, it was always his sign that ended up being placed back in the sacred spot by the road, while mine stayed tucked away in some random corner of the garage. But we all remember the outcome of election night. Let's just say my husband was quick to remove his sign from his side of the driveway the day after the election, when Romney officially became an also-ran. What a pity.

People say to me all the time, "I could never be married to my political opposite! Doesn't it drive you crazy?" The answer is: yes. It drives me crazy. But his snoring, his messes, and his pajamas all over the floor also drive me nuts. We've simply decided that this is not a deal breaker for us.

There are some good things that have come out of this too. I don't think my political beliefs would be half as strong if I had married someone who thinks just like me. Knowing that my husband and I are inevitably going to be debating the next big hot topics has motivated me to become more politically aware and really examine where I stand. I mean, think about it. You have to stay on your toes if you're going to be facing off with the opposing side at the dinner table.

I'm also proud that we've created an atmosphere in our house where people are welcome to discuss their beliefs. Nothing makes me more nervous than people who believe politics are not to be talked about. Of course they should be talked about! Our kids are more politically aware than many other kids because they hear us talking about politics all the time. And as an added bonus, they get to hear both sides of the issues. We joke about making our kids decide which side of the aisle they stand on by age five. But when it really does come time for them to decide, I feel confident that they'll be well educated on both sides, so they can make the best choice for themselves—and vote Democrat. (Or maybe not, *gasp!*)

It isn't easy being married to your political opposite. Nope, it's never easy, but it's always interesting. I hold out legitimate hope that I will someday convince my husband to come to his senses and see things my way. I just need to keep chipping away at him. But until then, we will continue to wage our political war passive aggressively out in front of our house every four years. For the record, I'm going to make "His" and "Hers" markers to accompany each of our lawn signs in 2016. I mean, if you're going to be obnoxious, you might as well take it to the next level, *right?*

MARIE BOLLMAN IS THE VOICE BEHIND MAKE YOUR OWN DAMN Dinner. She's a former Special Education teacher turned stay-at-home mom of three from Minnesota. She is wife to a work-traveling husband, a minivan monarch, and quite possibly the world's worst cook. Her writing has been featured on Felicity Huffman's What The Flicka?, BlogHer, and in the anthology, *The Mother of All Meltdowns.*

Don't Spill the Beer, Dear

By Julia Arnold

IT HAD BEEN SIX WEEKS SINCE I BROUGHT MY SECOND child, my daughter, kicking and screaming into the world. *Six* weeks—that magic number that men everywhere look forward to and women dread. My six-week follow-up gynecologist appointment was that morning across town, screwing up all hopes of squeezing in a real nap or any type of rest for the day.

I dutifully dragged my newborn baby and my active two-year-old son to a busy, cold doctor's office, where after working hard to prevent meltdowns in both children in the waiting room, I endured the fun of a freezing metal speculum while holding my six-week-old baby. (Yes, I held her the *entire exam* because she screamed every time I tried to put her down. Try to insert *anything* down there in a mother who is enduring the screams of her newborn baby, and well, holding the baby was the only reasonable solution.)

After the long, incredibly uncomfortable exam, my children and I made the drive back to our house, all of us taking turns fussing and crying the entire car ride. We were a motley crew, I'm sure. The following hours went by slowly and languidly, as they typically do in those endless, sleep-deprived, hormonal post-baby days. When the blessed point of bedtime for my son finally arrived, which had to have been about twenty hours later, my husband put him down to sleep, while my daughter happily stayed up for her first nighttime nursing session.

Did I mention that it also happened to be our five-year wedding anniversary? Well, it was. And remember the six-week post-baby rule? There were some definite expectations on the docket that night. The nurse who did my exam thought it was hilarious. I chuckled right along with her, but didn't share her enthusiasm. At all.

My husband and I situated our baby in her bouncy seat, while we stood at the kitchen counter hunched over paper plates, eating another unnamed casserole I had defrosted that morning. Then I remembered something wonderful: there was a cold beer in the fridge with my name on it—my favorite kind that I had truly missed for those long nine months. Things were looking up.

Is it bad that a single, lonely beer was the best part of my day—that dreaming about cracking open that beer and taking a good swig brought me tremendous joy? Soon I was starting to relax and almost enjoy myself a little that evening. It is possible I even exhaled.

Then I heard—

CLACK. Glug, glug, glug.

My husband had knocked over my beer. My cherished, well-deserved beer was pouring out its delightfully fizzy contents over our entire kitchen counter and quickly cascading into a sticky mess onto the kitchen floor.

"Oh my god! *Really? You knocked it over? That's mine!*" So few things felt all mine at this point. Clearly, this beer was one of those things.

"Here, take mine," he offered, quickly reaching for a towel. It wasn't the same. Irrational, sure, but still. He spilled *my* beer. I wanted MINE back.

Dumping the rest of my dinner in the trash, I grabbed his half-drunk beer and trudged up the stairs with my tiny, hungry-yet-again daughter, ready to watch old episodes of *The Big Bang Theory* as I nursed the last beer in the house and my baby.

Several minutes elapsed. My husband didn't follow. I started feeling guilty, but not that guilty.

Alas, it is our anniversary, I pictured him thinking as I heard his heavy footsteps finally come up the stairs. He quietly came into our room and blankly watched Sheldon from *The Big Bang Theory* comically espouse his own virtues. I fed the baby with my teeth clenched and my shoulders up by my ears. *Is this our life now? Just five years following that happy, romantic day?* I braved a glance at him. I felt a pit in my stomach. *Who would talk first?*

I was the mean one, I knew that, but I've never been good at handling conflict, especially when it was clearly all my fault. I usually employ what is widely considered to be the least healthy option when facing an argument: avoidance. But again, the word "anniversary" stubbornly hung above our heads.

"So, uh, are we going to need to do it since it's our anniversary and all?" I finally mumbled, attempting a bit of humor, and taking a sip of the room temperature, no-longer-desirable beer. Looking back, I can see how few statements could be less romantic and endearing than mine.

"Could you at least apologize?" he sighed, not really looking at me. "I understand if you snap, but could you at least say you're sorry? I mean, I spilled a *beer*, and you yelled at me."

He was right. Was I really so undone that I would let a beer ruin our night? "Okay, I'm sorry, it's just that Oh ... my ... *god*, I had a long, exhausting, lonely day. I focused on two little people's needs all day long. Then, I had this one drink ... one that quickly became The Best Beer of All Time. But, okay, you're right. I'm sorry."

I'm still embarrassed by the way I acted that night. It was a *beer*, for crying out loud. I suppose it shows the extent to which mothers struggle emotionally and physically when recovering from childbirth and learning how to take care of their babies while also taking care of themselves. It is no small feat, but move forward we must.

Being that it was the six-week mark and my husband is a numbers guy, he soon shrugged it off and didn't hold a grudge. He knew we had to move on if we were going to get it on.

JULIA ARNOLD LIVES IN THE TWIN CITIES WITH HER WONDERFUL husband and two small children. She writes with humor and honesty about the less glamorous side of motherhood on her blog, Frantic Mama. In her world, the counter is always sticky and the floor is never clean. Her essays have been featured on What The Flicka?, Mamalode, Scary Mommy, and Mamapedia.

By Kevin Zelenka

Five-Second Rule Warfare

By Kevin Zelenka

I PRIDE MYSELF ON BEING A BIT OF A FOODIE. IT'S A VERY small amount of pride as I'm just an okay cook and know only an average amount of food trivia and techniques. I do about 95 percent of the cooking in our house and even made baby food for my twin sons when they were younger. But a male Julia Child I am not.

My wife, on the other hand, is great at making reservations. (Just kidding!) She does have her specialties, but she stopped fighting me for control of the kitchen. Could I make it a season on *Top Chef*? Probably not. Nor could I make it very far on *The Next Food Network Star* because I have what you would call a face for radio. However, I still like to believe I know more than a good share of men when it comes to cooking. So every once in a while, I go crazy in the kitchen. Sometimes my craziness even spills out into the backyard where the grill sits.

Most of my culinary creations happen when we have friends and family over for dinner. I've hosted "slider parties," made fancy crab and avocado salads for my wife's annual girls' trips, and put dishes in front of my in-laws that they ate to be polite but probably wouldn't have tried on their own. (Think tuna tartar on mini crostini as an appetizer and grilled scallops with a mango-jalapeno salsa for the main course.) They know me pretty well by now, but at the time of the five-second rule warfare, they probably thought I was trying to kill them.

One evening, we had my wife's parents over for buffalo burgers. It was an off kind of day. I'm sorry, when I say "off," what I mean is that I wanted to scream my head off, jump off a bridge, and my wife of less than a year was ready to tell me to F-off and look for a divorce lawyer.

My wife and I had been dealing with an issue: a letter we received earlier that day.

It was a letter from one of my least favorite government agencies—the IRS.

Are there three letters in the world that strike terror in the hearts of men more than these? (If you're thinking PMS, you're braver than I am!)

My beautiful wife was not the first to snag me—just the first to tame me. I had been married once before. It seems that my past had come back to haunt me. Through this letter, I learned that my ex-wife, who was in charge of filing our taxes, had failed to file my quarterlies for the years I worked as an independent contractor. Now here I was years later with my new wife and my new life and an old bill that I thought was paid with a ton of interest added on to boot. The letter we received was *supposed* to be an income tax refund check for about five thousand and five hundred dollars. Instead, it was a "thank you for the nice payment" letter from the folks in Washington, D.C. and a reminder that I still owed about twelve thousand dollars more. Not only did I find out that the government wanted money from me and was going to do whatever it saw fit to get it, but my bride of less than a year immediately went silent.

My wife and I spent the next four or five tense hours going about our business and doing anything in our power to not speak to each other. I was as shocked as she was, and whether she chose to believe it or not, I was just as angry. Of course, I couldn't communicate my anger toward my first wife so it seemed like I was projecting my frustration at her. And that just made things worse. The reciprocal silent treatment over a situation beyond our control was the go-to result. I had never wanted someone to show up at our door as badly as I wanted my wife's parents to do at that very moment.

When they finally arrived, we all spent some time talking about the letter and what we were going to do to send the Devil a check for over ten grand. Her mother and I held the same thought, "It is what it is." Bite the bullet and move on.

They offered to loan us the money, which really showed me the type of people they were. I had only known them for a few years, and our visits were short. Here I was, the man who stole their daughter from them and took her away from her home state to live in Las Vegas, and they were willing to write a check to help us with a situation that happened in my previous life. We thanked them for the offer, but graciously declined. We had the money in savings. It was just tough to part with a good portion of the safety net we had been building together.

With that behind us, a glass of wine in hand, and the table on the back patio set, it was time for me to fire up the grill. I was ready to cook! Anyone who knows food knows that the leaner the meat, the longer it takes to grill. Fat heats up quickly, so a burger that is made with 80 percent meat to 20 percent fat is going to cook quicker than a burger that only has 7 percent fat. Buffalo is very lean meat, which was on the menu that night.

All of the side dishes were laid out down the center of the patio table. There was a gentle breeze coming in from somewhere. The candles I had placed around the patio provided exactly the right ambiance, that comfortable, intimate dining setting without being creepy. The wine was flowing nicely, softening any rough edges of attitudes and tempers from our earlier ordeal.

At that moment, my biggest concern was to offset the train wreck of an afternoon with a successful dinner that evening. *Balance is key.* I was also concentrating on not serving my mother- and father-in-law overcooked buffalo burgers that ran me over ten dollars per pound. The patties had been pre-made, and they were thick. I carefully seasoned one side of the massive slabs of ground meat and gently placed them on the grates. I could hear the wonderful sizzle of the beast as it touched the hot metal. My inner chef was whispering in my ear, repeating something I saw on a television program once: *"Season the side that touches the grill first ... and don't season too early as you don't want the salt to rob you of the juiciness of the meat."*

After a few minutes, I decided it was time to work on side two. I sprinkled the raw meat facing me with salt and pepper and tenderly turned them over, hoping that I'd not cooked them too long. *Must ... not ... ruin ... burgers,* I repeated to myself. I stared at the grill marks from side one and was almost mesmerized by the sound of the propane doing its job on our dinner.

After a few minutes, I called my dinner party to my side with plates in hand and gingerly set each burger on an awaiting bun. This would be the grilling event to remember. These burgers were going to fix whatever had been broken earlier in the day. Mine was the last to leave the grill, and after putting it on my plate next to the homemade potato salad and sliced tomatoes, I turned off the grill and walked excitedly to my place at the table. A few bites, a couple of looks exchanged, and I could tell there was definitely something wrong. I took a bite of the burger before me, and staring at me from between the flakey crust of the Kaiser roll was raw meat with just a hint of browning around the edges.

They were not the beautiful medium to medium rare for which I was hoping (make that praying)—these were one step above raw. I had been so worried about over-cooking, I never gave any thought to checking the temperatures to make sure I didn't serve buffalo tartar to my guests! I was defeated. All of the excited energy I felt only minutes before had escaped my body, and a broken man stood up to see whether I needed to put them back on the grill—or whether the ketchup and mustard could somehow hide my culinary failure. My father-in-law was fine with his, and I figured I could probably eat mine as well. My mother-in-law and wife both decided that a couple more minutes on the grill probably couldn't hurt.

I started the grill once again, happy that at least my back was to my audience. Two patties of wild game hit the fire for a few more minutes per side. The flames below were as warm as my flesh. I could feel the heat on my cheeks, and it wasn't the smoke from between the grates causing it, it was the flush of embarrassment. My hands shook with nervousness as I returned my mother-in-law's dinner to her plate. After a bite, she gave me the nod of approval, and I turned to retrieve my wife's burger. I picked it up with the spatula, and, as I turned back toward her, the thick sizzling mass failed to move as fluidly as I did, and we all watched as her buffalo jumped from flipper to floor.

My wife said, "That's fine. Just pick it up, and I'll eat it." The words were a slap in the face, already marked with the lines of frustration.

"You'll what?" I asked, confused and totally taken aback by her remark. When I say "floor," I don't really mean floor as in clean hardwood just washed before company came. I mean floor as in concrete, outside, dirty, dusty, and exposed to the elements. I could have said "from flipper to ground," but it didn't sound as nice.

"You will not eat it off the ground. Are you crazy? It's dirty. We're outside."

"No, it's okay. Just give it to me," she said.

"You won't eat raw meat in a burger, but you'll eat one that was on filthy concrete?" I questioned.

In the end, I tossed the one that got away into the trash, put my own back on the grill for a bit, and forfeited it to save my marriage. I had lost my appetite as quickly as it seemed to me my wife had lost her mind.

Looking back now, I know that she said she would indulge in the dirt-covered bison in order to keep peace and move the evening along. She was as mentally exhausted as I had been and really wanted nothing more than the night to be over—tainted meat or not. We survived the next hour before her parents left, and after cleaning up we both went to bed. It was a night that we didn't talk about until a couple years later, when her parents moved here.

We were grilling at their new home, and I had just come in from outside. I asked who wanted cheese on their burgers. After counting the show of hands, I looked at my mother-in-law to get her attention and then asked my wife, "Do you want me to drop it on the patio for you?"

We all erupted into laughter, and thankfully can still laugh about the five-second rule warfare to this day.

KEVIN ZELENKA IS A FREELANCE WRITER AND THE STAY-AT-HOME dad of fraternal twin toddlers. With his sons he loves reading, working on new words and songs, and taking them to meet-ups with other dads in the area. In what little time he carves out for himself, he enjoys golf, cigars, and writing on his blog, Double Trouble Daddy. A strong voice against how fathers are depicted in advertisements and a firm advocate of the importance of dads in their children's lives, he also enjoys cooking, gardening, and spending quality time with his wife both with and without his boys.

Car Care in the Lover's Lane

By Ginny Marie

W HEN I WAS SINGLE, I DREAMED OF THE DAY THAT I would meet a kind and loving man. I also wanted someone who would take care of my car. I was independent, had a good job, lived on my own, and felt I could do just about anything I set my mind to do, but I hated taking my car into the shop for service. I disliked feeling stupid about what makes a car work. I imagined that my car would break down on me and leave me stranded at the side of the road. What would I do then? Who would I call for help? When I finally met the one, I knew that he would take care of my automotive needs.

I bought my first car after starting my first teaching job, prior to being married. I loved my used 1988 silver Buick Skyhawk. A car was the first major purchase that I had ever made, and it was all mine. Since it was all mine, I had to take care of my car. My dad taught me how to check the oil and pump gas, but that was about all I knew about vehicle care. I took it in for regular oil changes and maintenance and hoped for the best.

One day it started acting funny, as I drove to my parents' house for the weekend. My dad wasn't home to give me advice. My mom and I decided that the battery needed charging, so I should drive around the neighborhood—which was a very bad idea. Mom knew as much about cars as I did, which was practically zilch. We ventured into a land that no car-care-non-expert should ever roam.

The Skyhawk stopped dead in the middle of a busy intersection. My handy-dandy 1990s car phone had to be plugged into the car battery, so calling for help wasn't an option. I left the car where it was, blocking traffic, and ran to the nearest gas station to plead for help. I learned that day that a car has something called an alternator, which helps charge the battery, and my alternator was dead. Driving around the neighborhood wouldn't charge the battery if the alternator didn't work. Ooops.

For the most part, however, it was a good car, and it lasted a long time. I saved up my money for a down payment on a new car. After a few years, I bought a brand-new, dark-green Subaru Legacy. I was thrilled to be the owner of a new car and was sure I would never have any problems with it. One day, however, I goofed again.

When parking the car in the garage of the house I rented, I didn't notice that I had left the door ajar. The dome light stayed on all night, and when I went to leave for work the next morning, the car wouldn't start. Just like that, the battery was dead. I imagined my second-grade students arriving at a dark and quiet classroom, not knowing the whereabouts of their teacher. I panicked. Fortunately, the school wasn't very far away. I called the school office, and the gym teacher came to pick me up.

As time went on, I finally met the man who would eventually become my husband. I soon discovered that after working ten-hour days, he barely had time to take his own car in for oil changes, much less take care of mine. Not only did he not have time for my car, but some of our first arguments happened in the car. I suppose our exchanges weren't even long enough to merit calling them "fights." Ed and I had a tendency to bicker. We'd snap at each other, get irritated, maybe go off to sulk for a while, and then forget about the whole thing.

One night, we were driving home after eating a nice dinner at a restaurant. The weather was turning bad, and it was sleeting outside. Ed was driving through the parking lot toward a busy intersection. The driveway sloped downward. Ed hit the brakes, but the car didn't stop. We were heading straight through the red light.

"You need to stop!" I yelled, as the car continued to slide forward.

"I'm well aware of that! Don't you think I'm trying to stop?" he snapped back. The car slowly slid to a stop just beyond the white line as cars rushed by, almost brushing our front bumper.

Another time, we were in Yellowstone National Park on vacation. In order to get to the other side of the park, we had to drive on a mountainous road. I'm a flatlander from Illinois. You can't get much flatter than the farm fields of Iroquois County. As I looked out the window, the side of the mountain dropping away into nothingness seemed to get steeper and steeper. The two-lane road seemed extremely narrow and twisty, and there wasn't much of a shoulder. I held my breath. I closed my eyes. I bit my tongue. I couldn't stand it! "Can't you drive farther away from the edge?" I said between clenched teeth, as I fiercely gripped the armrest.

"Would you like me to have a head-on collision?" he tersely replied. We spent the rest of the drive in a stony silence until we reached our destination. We didn't plunge off the mountainside to our deaths after all.

Eventually, Ed and I married, had a couple of kids, and owned a typical family minivan. All of my expectations of having my husband take care of my car had long disappeared. I was available more often than he was, so I took care of the van and also insisted on buying an American Automobile Association (AAA) membership, just in case.

Last fall, I began working more hours at my job teaching preschool. Classes were just beginning, and one day, I had a two-hour break for lunch. The van was acting funny: the automatic rear door wasn't lifting up smoothly. I didn't think much about it, and ran to Walgreens for an errand.

Will I ever learn?

When I came out of Walgreens, the van wouldn't start because the battery was dead. First, I called AAA. Then I called my husband at work. I left a detailed message with the receptionist, telling her I was having car trouble and that I needed Ed to call me back as soon as possible.

It was a beautiful day. At the edge of the parking lot, there was a nice grassy area, and I sat down under a tree. I had an estimated time when AAA was going to arrive, but my husband had still not returned my call. I tried to relax and enjoy the nice weather, despite being stuck in a Walgreens' parking lot.

The AAA truck arrived, and the mechanic told me that my battery was corroded. He could jump it for me now, or I would have to buy a battery from him and he would install it. I knew how easy it was to install a new battery even though I'd never done it myself. Would Ed want me to buy a new battery and have the mechanic take care of the problem? I had no answers, because I had not heard from him—at all! *What was going on with my husband?*

By this time, I really needed to get back to work, so I decided to hell with it and had the mechanic install a new battery. When I got home and asked Ed why he hadn't called his stranded wife back, he said he simply forgot about calling. *Really?* How could he forget about me? At least he agreed with my decision to have the new battery installed on the spot. It made life easier for both of us.

The last time my car needed service, I finally resigned myself to taking caring of it myself. I called the dealership and arranged for a shuttle to take my daughters and me to where we needed to be for the day. We went out with a friend and her daughter for lunch, and afterwards took the girls to a playground. After they had played for a while, my friend drove us back to the shop to pick up our car. I didn't call my husband once. I just took care of the service visit myself.

Just recently, my husband asked me to switch cars with him. He wanted to drive the van to work and have me take his car into the shop to have new tires installed. I wonder if he ever dreamed that he would meet a woman who would take care of his car. I highly doubt it, but it happened anyway.

While I still don't like taking our vehicles into the shop, it's very practical for me to get the job done. Go ahead and order those Bridgestones, Ed. I'll take care of it!

SINCE THE YELLOWSTONE INCIDENT, ED HAS DRAGGED GINNY Marie to National Parks all over the country, including Death Valley. Any bickering that occurred during that trip was due to the unbearable desert heat. Ginny Marie blogs at Lemon Drop Pie and is a contributor to *The Mother of All Meltdowns*. Ginny was also named a BlogHer Voice of the Year in 2013 and has been featured on BlogHer and QueenLatifah.com. One of her personal essays

By Ginny Marie

was published in *Chicken Soup for the Soul: The Dating Game* and she contributes to WatchUsGrow.org under her IRL-name, Christa Grabske.

Ode to a Kiss

By Mike Reynolds

"HONESTY AND TRUST ARE THE KEYS TO A STRONG RELA-tionship that lasts for many years and helps couples survive all the ups and downs that come with raising children."—Many smart people who have never met my wife and me.

Now, this isn't to say that we don't trust each other or that we aren't honest all the time. Sure, we sneak chocolates late at night without telling the other, but we also leave the wrappers hidden in plain sight so that the other one knows to sneak one the next night.

Really, we're like everyone else with our little secrets. But we're also very forthcoming in admitting that our entire relationship is based on an argument neither of us will ever give up on and which will threaten the sanctity of our marriage forever—who initiated our first kiss.

For more than ten years, each of us has insisted that we were the one who instigated the first of the eight kisses we've ever shared as a couple, and for more than ten years, I truly believe that both of us honestly thinks we're in the right. I know I'm right when I say it is me, and I know she thinks she's right when she says it is her.

So as we go through parenthood deciding on using cloth diapers or disposable ones, on co-sleeping or having our children sleep on their own, on educating them in Catholic schools or public schools, and never heating our debates past a medium simmer, it takes but a mention of the moment outside my wife-to-be's front door that fateful night years ago to bring us to a full boil.

On those rare occasions when we find ourselves out on a date night, we harken back to the same conversation over and over again.

"I love you more now than I did ten years ago," I'll tell her, cupping her face in my hands, admiring just how beautiful and smart she is. "I'm so lucky to have met you and don't want to picture a life without you."

"And I've never been happier. I love you too," she'll say, bringing tears to my eyes. "You're smart and kind of funny, and I feel like I really lucked out."

"I couldn't ever have imagined this moment all those years ago when I kissed you on your front steps," I'll say, wiping my tears away.

And then there will be a slight shifting of her body and an unwelcome uneasiness will come over the night. My tears dry up as I realize the discussion I was trying to avoid is about to begin. For the seventeenth time.

"Wait," she'll say, gently pushing herself away from me, so she can see me more clearly (this argument is always better with eye contact). "Do you mean the second time we kissed?"

"No, the first one. At your house. When I pulled you in and kissed you gently. Remember when the angels tooted their horns?"

"That was me. I was the one who kissed you first. You would have rambled on about raccoons until the sun came up. Then you'd have waited longer, probably until you had sweat through your shirt. I kissed you."

"We're not doing this again, *are we?*"

"I don't know, Mike. Are you ready to admit that I was the one who kissed you first? That it was me who leaned in bravely and put our relationship on firm ground?"

"I'm not, because it's too important to the future of our children that I stay true to what I believe in. That I remain confident enough in myself to be able to take on a bully like yourself."

"Yada yada."

"Yes, yada yada."

Our battles have become regular enough that if we sense a conversation with another couple turning to the topic of how the two of us met, we feel obligated to warn them that at some point our partner will lie to them. Yes, we call each other liars, and yes, it's for the good of our relationship.

It can be awkward sometimes, living with a partner who refuses to acknowledge my gentle approach to our first kiss, but I believe that in a very roundabout way it makes us stronger as parents:

1) It makes us less susceptible to the exaggerations (lies) children tell.

2) We're very good at storytelling time.

3) We frequently extend bedtime so that we both have equal time to explain our sides of the story to our children individually.

I know this argument will come to a head at some point (my money is on at either a graduation or a marriage if my kids decide to pursue either), but for now we're just fine with letting the chasm between our stories grow.

Right now, we at least have similar memories of the moment, just differing opinions of who moved first. But as our children drive us crazier and as our minds just naturally get more muddled, I expect our first-kiss story to become part of family legend.

In time, it will become a campfire story our children's children will tell their children about the time their great-grandparents had their first kiss—how they were the first humans to ever kiss on the planet Mars and how from that kiss, the hover boards predicted in *Back to the Future* were finally realized. They'll talk about how it brought back the dinosaurs and made lions and elk best friends.

In time, nobody will remember who kissed whom first because it will no longer be part of the story. They'll remember that we raised great storytellers with great imaginations who grew up to tell tales that kept people entertained.

First kisses are overrated anyway. We do remember who asked whom on their first date, and for that we have no debate. Like the first kiss, it was me.

MIKE REYNOLDS IS AN OTTAWA-BORN-AND-RAISED HUSBAND AND father of two. He's mildly obsessed with making sure his daughters says "daddy and mommy" and not "mommy and daddy" (with little success) and with ensuring his daughters know they're both one-of-a-kind. He also writes bedtime stories with his daughters and shares stories about the trials and tribulations of raising two girls after growing up in a house full of boys at Puzzling Posts.

Red Light Rodeo, Couples-Style

By Leigh-Mary Hoffmann

HERE ON LONG ISLAND, NEW YORK, WE HAVE THESE fancy red-light cameras designed to ~~make money for the state~~ capture an image (and video) of your car and license plate in the event that you go through a red light or do not stop for a *full three seconds* before making a right on red. If you commit either of these crimes, an eighty-dollar ticket will be issued. It doesn't matter who was driving the car at the time the infraction was made. The ticket is sent to whoever owns the car, as there is no way to prove who was behind the wheel at the time (though the ticket is date- and time-stamped, so you can reasonably determine who is actually at fault).

It was a Tuesday afternoon when I arrived home from work and checked the mail. I found a few of my favorite catalogs, the latest issue of *People* magazine, some bills, and *IT*.

Unfortunately, this wasn't my first red light rodeo, and I knew exactly what the upper left hand corner of that envelope meant. All I could do was open it and hope that the car in the photo was black, which would mean it was my husband's car. No such luck. It was my people mover, my gold minivan, my red-light ticket. I checked the video tape (the ticket gives you a link to see the violation live), and it was true, I *slowly* rolled through the light to make a right on red (and I know it was me driving because my husband was working at the time of the incident, and he doesn't take my car to work). There was not another car in sight, but I did not come to a full stop for a full three seconds, so, BOOM, eighty bucks—gone.

When my husband came home that evening, I told him about the ticket.

"I'm not surprised," he snickered. Despite the eighty-dollar hit, I think he found a touch of satisfaction that I was called out for my driving—of which he is not a fan.

Snide remarks, in a somewhat playful way, were made throughout the evening, including lots of unnecessary emphasized references to the words "stop," "red," and "ticket."

Can you STOP and pick up milk tomorrow?

Do you know if my RED shirt is clean?

Did you get a TICKET at the dry cleaners?

Please STOP doing that.

You get the idea.

Really, sweetie? Really? Just you wait.

As if the payback gods were on my side, when I took in the mail that Friday afternoon there were more bills (of course!) and another envelope with that dreaded return address. Please. NO! I never hide anything from my husband, but if I got another red-light ticket—just three days after the first—I may have had to spare myself the "I told you so" speech and tuck it in a tampon box. I doubt he would find it there!

I was almost as nervous as I was opening a thin envelope from the college admissions office over twenty years ago. A thin envelope was never good news, but hot damn and hallelujah, the car in the picture in *this* thin envelope was black. A black Civic. A black Civic, as in my husband's car.

Touché.

Tou-freakin-ché.

Fast forward two hours: "Welcome home honey. How was your day?" I cheerfully greeted my self-proclaimed excellent-driver husband with a kiss hello.

"Good. How about you? Did we get any mail?" he asked.

I don't know why we both always ask if we got any mail. Mail stinks. No one ever sends us surprise checks or gifts. For the most part, it's just junk mail or bills. Well, except for this day. (Insert maniacal laugh.)

"Just some bills. Oh, and you got something else," I said. "Here you go."

I handed him the envelope, and he nervously smiled. Not because he knew we were now out even more hard-earned money—that part sucks—but because he knew I wouldn't have been so eager to hand over the envelope unless this ticket was for his driving mistake, not mine.

He tried everything he could to determine whether it was me driving his car. According to the paperwork, the ticket was issued on a Saturday, and we were both home that day. He took out a magnifying glass. He watched the video. He watched it again. *And again.* But there was no way to determine who was driving.

Even though I often use his car on the weekends, so I don't have to use the minivan, it was totally him driving. I'm sure of it. Maybe.

Luckily, our arguments are few and far between. When we do disagree, it is usually because we are both stubborn, sarcastic smart asses. Oh, and *each of us* is *always* right. Well, *I am* anyway. Except when I'm not—but we don't need to talk about that.

But in this red-light case, the proof is in the pudding; which, in this instance, is in the license plate.

Moral of this story: stop a full three seconds before making a right on red. And always be the first person to get to the mail.

LEIGH-MARY HOFFMANN IS A "MY LIFESTYLE" BLOGGER FROM Long Island, New York, juggling a family, a job, and a busy, crazy life. She tells it like it is—the good, the bad, and the ugly—and tries to keep a smile on her face and laughter in her life. Her story reads like a cross between the lyrics of a feel-good country song and the script from an "I can't believe this happened to her" Lifetime Movie of the Week. She invites you to visit her blog, Happily Ever Laughter Blog, and share in the laughter.

A Hypothetical Situation

By Lynn Shattuck

LIKE MANY OF OUR ARGUMENTS, THIS ONE OCCURRED *EN route* to one of my husband's family functions.

"But why?" I pouted. We were just rounding the corner of Portland's Back Cove. The cityscape stretched out in the background, a scattering of brick buildings and trees. I took in the sight of the city I loved, but it didn't really register—my eyes gobbled it up while my brain stayed agitated.

My husband, Scott, his arms tense on the steering wheel, gave me his patented are-you-out-of-your-effing-mind? look.

"Seriously?" he asked, his calico-hued eyebrows reaching toward the top of his head.

"Yes. I've *always* wanted a biracial baby."

"No. Just, no."

"Are you racist or something?" I asked, raising my own eyebrows in an arched accusation.

He shook his head. "I'm not racist. But *neither of us is black.*"

I sighed. The man had a point.

At this juncture, four years into our relationship, I was well on my way to learning that dredging up hypothetical arguments was a recipe for disaster.

Once, while snuggling in bed after watching a movie, I was rubbing his belly. It was early in our relationship, and I was still in awe that we had found each other. "Can I please get in your belly?" I blurted. It just slipped out.

"No," he said, as quickly as I had asked. "You may not."

"Why not?" I asked, still stroking the fine hairs on his stomach. His rejection of my impossible request not only offended me, it struck a match under my desire to somehow, against all odds, get into his belly.

"Because," he said. He offered no physiological reason, and this enraged me.

"I can't believe you won't let me get in your belly!" I pulled my hand away.

"Chill out, baby," he responded.

"Fine. I would've let you get in my belly, but there's no way that's happening now," I sulked.

"That's okay. I don't want to get in your belly."

"What in the hell is wrong with my belly?" I whined.

The argument finally faded, but it wasn't the only one of its kind.

"Would you still think I was hot if I lost all my limbs?" I'd asked him one time after he'd made an inappropriate joke about Heather Mills, who at the time was married to Paul McCartney.

He'd stared at me for a breath, then replied firmly, "I'm not going to have this conversation with you."

"What if I was morbidly obese?"

Again, he shut me down. My bait was left dangling; not even a nibble. Scott had once told me he'd follow me to the ends of the earth. *Why was I asking him to drag my pudgy torso along too?*

But back to Portland's Back Cove.

"But biracial babies are beautiful," I whispered guiltily. I realized it sounded the same as, "but that opal ring is beautiful," or "but that zillion-dollar cottage on the beach is beautiful." The stink of low tide seeped into our car, and I stared out the window at the beige flats of the cove. People jogged around it looking miserable, and I briefly wondered if it was the running or the stench that made them appear so unhappy.

"Hey, you're Jewish!" my husband exclaimed.

"Sort of," I agreed. My mother's mother was Jewish, so technically it was true. However, meager attempts to light a menorah in the shadow cast by the present-laden Christmas tree was as Jewish as my family had ever gotten. "What's your point?"

"So we *will* have biracial babies," he smirked.

On another recent drive to one of his family get-togethers, we'd had a blowout about whether Jewishness was a religion or an ethnicity. I'd won that argument after some frantic Internet research to prove my point. However, my husband had just turned my win into his own. Victory had stabbed me in the uterus.

"That's not what I mean," I said.

I glanced at his profile, strong and handsome. Our disagreement had started innocently, with my offhand remark. But throughout the course of our conversation, as was my pattern, I'd swallowed the argument whole, convincing myself that this ridiculousness mattered. Seriously, would he think I was still hot if I was obese or limbless? Why, in the name of all that is right and holy, couldn't I get in his belly? And dammit, why couldn't we have mocha-skinned, sapphire-eyed little muffins?

But underneath my overactive, argumentative imagination was a general anxiety about having children. I had just turned thirty-two, and my ovaries were pulsing. Sometimes I rubbed my flat stomach, imagining it blooming round and full. But Scott wasn't sure he was ready to be a dad. At twenty-eight, my young spouse wasn't confined by a biological clock—he still had decades of seed-spreading time ahead of him, while my fertility window was slowly sliding shut. And I was becoming resentful. And scared.

We drove in silence for several minutes, leaving the runners, walkers, and bikers of Back Cove behind us as our car merged onto the highway.

I huffed. I leaned my body as close to the door as possible, and as far away from my husband as possible.

"Why crabbin'?" he asked. Crabbin' was our shorthand for the "crab maneuver"—a sideways move I'd perfected when my feelings were hurt. Instead of looping our ankles together and nestling in his armpit at bedtime (since he refused to let me in his belly), I'd scuttle over to my side of the bed, turning my face and vulnerable underside away from him, as if to ward off further harm.

"I don't know," I sighed. "Because you hurt my feelings."

"By saying we can't have a biracial baby? Because, like I said, neither of us is black?"

I stayed silent. *Because you're saying we can't have* our *baby,* I wanted to say. We drove on for several more minutes, the whoosh of the highway the only sound. I edged closer to the passenger-side door.

"Hey! I know!" he said suddenly.

"What?" I turned my body ever-so-slightly toward him, a spark of hope in my eyes.

"Find me a nice African-American girl, and I will reproduce with her." He smiled, proud of his stroke of genius. "I'll take one for the team," he added.

"Screw that. *I'll* take one for the team," I replied. "But then, I'm already pretty dark-skinned. So that might not produce the desired results," I admitted. It was at this point that I realized how insane I sounded. Nevertheless, I still resented his ability to stay calm and crack jokes while I was trapped in my own lunacy.

I took another deep breath. "This is ridiculous."

"You think?" he answered.

"I'm sorry. Let's just go and have a nice time with your family," I said. Which was ironic, since my social anxiety and inability to let go was the reason I started these bizarre arguments before gatherings.

"Sounds good to me," he said.

It's been eight years since our silly, and frankly, one-sided, argument. Eventually, I wore the man down and we produced two amazing kids, who *did* get in my belly. They both have gorgeous blue eyes, despite not being biracial.

My penchant for peculiar hypothetical conversations has disappeared. Perhaps I tamped it down with years of therapy. But more likely, it's because my life now overflows with irrational, outlandish disputes and requests. I have no time or energy to add more tomfoolery to the mix.

"Mama, what time is it?" my two-year-old daughter asks from her crib.

"It's bedtime, sweetie," I respond.

"No! Don't say that! Say it's morning time!" she hollers.

I take a deep breath, trying to figure out how to reason with a small, crazy person. It occurs to me that this might be how my husband used to feel during some of our conversations.

"It's actually bedtime," I say.

"NOOO! SAY IT'S MORNING TIME!" the tiny, adorable tyrant shrieks.

"How about I sing you a song?" I ask in a syrupy voice. *You are my sunshine, my only—"*

"NOOOOOOO!" she hollers, kicking her feet like a judo master. My attempts at distraction are failing. Frustration rises in my chest, red and bubbling.

Fortunately, at this point, Scott enters the room. Our bedtime routine is to each put one kid to bed, then switch to say goodnight to the other.

"Peace out," I blurt, while fleeing the room. He can take *this* one for the team.

As a mom of two young children, Lynn Shattuck attempts to balance diapers and laptops, yoga and running, and tucks as much writing as she can into the remaining nooks and crannies of her life. Besides writing for her blog, The Light Will Find You, she is a featured columnist at the elephant journal and blogs for The Huffington Post. Her writing has also appeared on Brain, Child and Mamalode.

Only I Can Talk About Me

By Jeff Bogle

IT WAS A JOKE! WELL, IT WAS JOKE-ISH IN THE WAY THAT margarine is butter-ish, and about as tasteful.

"Didn't I tell you never to talk about me?"

It's a fact that I was not then, and still am not today, keen on the idea that people I don't know might be talking about me when I am not present, but I would never attempt to stand in the way of such conversations taking place. It is a fact that I am an asshole, but I'm not that colossal of an asshole. And anyway, how could I possibly prevent people from talking about me? Had I figured out the secret, maybe I'd have tried to stop the chatter, but as I hadn't, I'm generally tolerant of me as conversation piece. So it was well within my personality make-up to blurt out a sarcastic quip, a verbal knifing with a smile, and a chuckle to my new lady friend. The thing is, those cuts still bleed, no matter the smile on your face or the humor in your heart. All the while, I thought it was a harmless butter knife, but my weapon proved far sharper. I learned this lesson the hard way.

"Didn't I tell you never to talk about me?"

We were driving Lulu, a beat-up 1989 Chrysler New Yorker, the burgundy-colored lemon that a shyster of a used car salesmen friend of the family pushed on her for twice what it was worth, which was closer to nothing than something. Thanks to a personal driving radius of roughly twenty-five miles, the car managed to get us around well enough. On this night, Lulu was carrying us from West Chester, a quaint college town we frequented because of the music-biz friends I had at the time, back to South Philadelphia, where we'd already shacked up together in my one-bedroom apartment after a mere three weeks of dating. Our relationship was a shiny toy just placed on an endcap, the site of which could make youngsters envious and parents groan. It was nearly too new to withstand such cynicism.

"Didn't I tell you never to talk about me?"

We were halfway home when she began to tell a story of a conversation she'd had earlier that day while at work, a story of a conversation about me, a story I'd never actually hear the beginning, middle, or end of because I had to squeeze in my funny. From the age of six or maybe eight, I've had to be the one who'd incite laughter, and on this night, as two young lovers drove back from a joyous night, as the bright lights of the big city emerged from above the suburban roadside canopy, as the traffic cleared out in front of us, I tried as per usual to be funny, even if it meant cutting my love off to inject a second voice where there should have been only a pair of listening ears. I still do this. Too often. I'm a very slow learner.

"Didn't I tell you never to talk about me?"

It took me too long to fully understand that the nine words I used were less the problem than the presumed bitterness with which they were spoken. It was a rare case in which being taken out of context would have helped the orator. In that exact moment, while a highly sensitive, twenty-year-old girl struggled to keep her head above water in a new relationship with a boy unlike any she'd met before, the exact rhetorical question of, "Didn't I tell you never to talk about me?" was about the meanest thing any lad could possibly have said to someone he was beginning to fall in love with—someone he was beginning to think about spending the rest of his life alongside.

I still don't know the entire story, the one she almost was able to start telling me that evening on the expressway late at night, but I know it was a simple and loving one about a conversation she had in which she excitedly had told her new co-workers about something sweet I'd said or done, or about the romantic dinner we'd shared using chop sticks for the first time together at the new Asian-fusion spot on South Street, or about how charming it was watching me methodically wrap Christmas gifts for my family, or about a kiss we'd stolen beneath a street lamp during a mid-winter snow shower.

She'd been biding her time, patiently waiting for the night's conversations with friends to draw to their natural conclusions and waiting for me to stop giddily talking about the indie-rock band I'd just discovered (this can often take a while), so that she could relay her story about, in essence, how much and how quickly she'd come to love me and how she'd shared a story that exemplified this love with her people at work. It wasn't a movie, but it could've easily been a sappy moment from a Hollywood blockbuster released in color the previous summer or in black and white forty years prior. The cinematic bliss of young love is timeless. The same is true of sheer stupidity.

"Didn't I tell you never to talk about me?"

So brittle is young love that any nine words sequenced in such a way and said with malice, perceived or real, can shatter it into a number of pieces so impossible to count as to never be reassembled: grains of sand on a beach that once formed a vase that once held a fragrant bouquet. I'd like to laugh with that young girl, who is now my wonderful wife, about the fact that we survived me and my ways—but that will never happen.

The wave I caused with those nine words nearly drowned us both. Fifteen years, a marriage, a pair of children, three cats, five cars, and many sticks of butter later, we still cannot fully laugh openly and honestly about that brief exchange in her old car. The memories of that drive on that evening float on driftwood sturdier than you'd ever imagine possible, on a sea that is calmer now but not exactly as smooth as, say, butter.

JEFF BOGLE IS AN AT-HOME DAD WHO WRITES HUMOROUSLY ABOUT parenting and all things childhood on his site, *Out With The Kids*. His work also frequently appears on *The Huffington Post* and *The Good Men Project*, among other print and online outlets.

He is married to an adorable redheaded gal and has two lovely little ladies who provide him with countless hours of humorous in-home entertainment, and who get to hear, see, and play with more cool stuff than you can possibly imagine. He considers himself one of the luckiest guys in the world, although he needs to be reminded of this fact from time to time.

Sans Souvenir

By Angela Godbout

THIS STORY IS A BIT BIZARRE, BUT IT'S 100 PERCENT true. My husband (at the time) and I had a nice little family with nice little jobs and a nice little house. But with all of the little niceties, we also had debt. Little vacations were nearly impossible, so the only way we could manage some time away was to take nice little, separate, mini vacations with our friends.

But even those rarely happened. For me anyway. The kids were never left out. We did everything for them and with them including day trips to the ocean or weekends at our family camp up north. My husband was an outdoorsy kind of guy, so he went on hunting and fishing trips as often as we could afford. The big duck hunt happened every year. Four-wheeler trips and fishing trips, when possible.

It wasn't his fault that I didn't ever go anywhere without the kids. My maternal instinct had convinced me early on that they couldn't function without me. I had fun with them, and they were never something that I needed a break from. It was life in general.

When one of us was actually blessed enough to leave the state, we always brought home souvenirs for the kids—at least something with the name of the state on it. We had to because, most likely, we would never be able to afford to go there again in our lives.

My husband had an opportunity to go to New York on a fishing trip. I was so excited. We had never visited New York, nor would we ever get there as a family. His trip really strapped us, but we went forward with the plans. My husband enjoyed the fishing trip of a lifetime. There wasn't a whole lot left over for gifts, but there was enough—we had built souvenirs into the budget.

The kids and I missed him, but we were so excited to see what he would bring back other than fish. Maybe a toy, or a glass, or a T-shirt, a key chain, something, anything. On the night he was to return home, the kids tried to wait up, but failed. They were sound asleep when Daddy came through the door. I was also in bed, but not yet sleeping.

He came in and snuggled with me while telling me stories about the trip. It sounded amazing. I couldn't wait to get the film developed to see the pictures. Then I asked him if he put the kids' gifts on the table for them or if they were still packed in a bag.

His face dropped into a frown. There hadn't been enough money to get them anything, he explained. I laughed. *No, really, where did you hide them?* He just stared at me. I knew at that moment that he was serious. Taking a deep breath, I tried being rational and asked what happened. Maybe a vehicle broke down or someone got robbed—by a very large, seven-foot man or posse of drag queens looking for a fight. Despite there being a group of men together on a fishing trip, it *was* New York. But, no, nothing like *that* happened. What did happen was a strip club.

It was like pulling teeth to actually get the truth out of his mouth. I'm pretty sure he would've preferred having teeth pulled without Novocain than to be sitting there with me at that moment. I flipped a freaking wig. I completely lost it. And my tirade went on for hours.

Really?

You couldn't have even had one less lap dance and even gotten the kids a friggin' shot glass from the club?

They wouldn't have cared.

You seriously came home from a once-in-a-lifetime trip with absolutely nothing to show for it?

Are you kidding me?

I was on my knees on the bed as he just sat there. I was yelling and bawling all at the same time. I was so shocked and hurt all at once. What would the kids think? They looked forward to the little surprises.

I'm not the type to freak out. I'm typically so calm and laid back that I was shocking myself. Where were these emotions coming from? My heart was broken for my babies and me. I was emotionally exhausted.

Then I was aroused. Without going into details, I succumbed to my feelings and ended up having the most amazing sex of my entire married life. We fell asleep and when I woke up, I lied to my children to protect their feelings and promised to make it up to them. And I did.

ANGELA GODBOUT IS THE FOUNDER AND HOST OF "FRaPS", WHICH stands for Family, Relationships, and Personal Situations. At FRaPS Angela offers support and guidance to families who have suffered, at some point, a major life event. She creates the perfect atmosphere to have open discussions, bonding, and healing. The relationships that form within FRaPS are amazing and will be cherished forever. When she isn't supporting and guiding her FRaPS community, she can be found spending time with her family and friends.

A Middle-Age Man and His Table

By Jenny Hills

MY HUSBAND AND I HAVE ALWAYS BEEN A BIT RELA-tionship challenged. While opposites attract, they also bicker, nag, and pick fights. We spent the first eight years of our marriage painfully overcoming our argumentative tendencies, established a no-fighting rule, and after not hearing, "I told you so" for six months straight, life was looking pretty good. That is until we started eating dinner in the living room, and I bought some TV trays.

When we first got married, I was a stickler for eating dinner the proper way: as a family, at the kitchen table. My somewhat traditional views were the byproduct of my own upbringing and my undying obsession with the formality and grandeur of yesteryear. I fantasized about feasting on homemade fare to the sounds of our children sharing the highlights of their day. My husband and I would look at each other adoringly, waiting for the moment when we could fall asleep in each other's arms. Although getting the kids to talk about their day was always a challenge and the looks of adoration were few and far in between, I was pretty good at assembling my family around the kitchen table most nights of the week.

However, as our children grew older, our evenings became cluttered with practices, evening runs to the grocery store, and homework battles. Consequently, we went from eating homemade meals at our handmade kitchen table to being squished together like sardines on the sofa while devouring cheap pizza off of paper plates. A busy schedule waits for no one, and my beloved old-fashioned dinnertime became the victim of our modern-family status.

Eating in the living room was primarily my husband's idea, and while I wasn't exactly a fan, I obliged. His job was physically draining and mentally demanding. Consequently, by the time everything else was taken care of and dinner was finally done, so was he. Not only did eating on the sofa give my husband some much-needed relaxation, it made me look good. I was doing my best to promote a peaceful marriage and didn't want to be labeled as disagreeable.

However, soon enough, the new routine began to annoy me, and I eventually found it impossible to enjoy dinner away from the kitchen table. The arrangement was messy, loud, and generally obnoxious. There had to be a better option than hoping and praying that my son didn't accidently elbow me, sending a plate of spaghetti and meat-balls onto my lap. Believe me; we had more close calls than I care to remember.

One day, while watching my favorite classic television show, I had an epiphany. The answer was right in front of my face. What would the nuclear family of yesteryear do? They would eat off TV trays, of course! In a retro frame of mind, I ordered a few folding tables, complete with trays that were covered in a faux-wood-grain contact paper. Tacky yet functional, I was hopeful that the tables would make dinnertime more enjoyable and tip my family off to the fact that I wasn't exactly enjoying our current arrangement. Plus, I was secretly excited at the prospect of adding a bit of nostalgia to our all-too-modern existence.

The trays arrived in a blaze of glory, and we were instant-ly addicted to their kitschy brand of utility. However, as the weeks went by, I noticed a disturbing trend: my husband wasn't putting his tray away after dinner. When the trays first arrived, I had explicitly explained that they were to be folded and returned to their proper place in the closet as soon as dinner was over. I wasn't about to let my living room become a permanent cafeteria. There had to be some boundaries!

Even more disturbing was that my husband started using his tray as an extension of the coffee table. By the time we went to bed each night, his tray housed no less than five glasses, a box of crackers, and a couple of cell phone chargers. One night I caught him rummaging around the house, collecting old magazines, some mints, and a puzzle. "What's that stuff?" I asked while he placed his treasures on the tray. "You know the tables are for eating, right?" "I know," he replied. "Just gathering a few things I might need for the night."

Apparently, that TV tray had aged my husband by about forty years. That's right, every night after the clock struck eight, he settled into his side of the sofa and didn't get up unless nature called. Hey, even that interruption could be alleviated with a little trip to the grocery store's personal care aisle.

Coincidentally, his television viewing habits changed as well. *Wheel of Fortune* replaced the football game, and we became one of the six families in town that watched the public access channel. His vision suddenly became poor, prompting the purchase of some reading glasses. I got a lot of bang for my buck with those TV trays. Little did I know, I actually purchased a time machine. Life was becoming a little too old fashioned for my liking.

To make matters worse, his tray was disgustingly dirty. While the other tables were wiped down each night, I stubbornly refused to take care of his. After nearly a decade of marriage, I had become a pro at being passive aggressive and wasn't about to stop now. Every night I put my tray away in a tizzy of anger, banging and slamming it instead of gently folding it per the manufacturer's directions.

Refusing to appear overtly disagreeable, I came up with an array of creative ways to express my disgust. I would incessantly ask my husband if he was done with any one of his many beverages or casually mention that the box of crackers shouldn't be left out overnight. Despite these exhaustive efforts, he just didn't get the hints. In fact, the lingering piles became so cumbersome that he started eating on his lap again. My anger was building by the second. I was ready to erupt.

A few weeks later, I came home to the foreign, captivating smell of homemade brownies. "Wow," I thought to myself. "Homemade baked goods! My husband is amazing."

Then I saw it.

There on his table were three mixing bowls, a carton of eggs, a box of brownie mix, a bottle of vegetable oil, and a collection of batter-covered utensils. All love was instantly lost, and the volcano blew.

"What on earth is that?" I shouted.

"What's what?" he replied. "What's your problem? I made brownies for you."

"You brownies for me? YOU made brownies for ME? I don't think so. You made YOURSELF brownies on your old-man table."

Oh. No. The words that had been trapped in my devious little mind finally escaped. I was a goner.

"My what? Did you say 'old-man table'?"

My son and the dog escaped to the den and took my dignity along with them. Now I was annoyed that he had made me so mad. All bets were off.

"Yes," I said, standing a little taller. I was going to win this battle. "You're like an old man with that table. The piles of stuff, the new glasses, the boring TV shows. I feel like I'm married to a grandpa!"

"Oh, well," he replied. "I see. I didn't know you felt that way. I like the tables. I thought the tables were a good thing for us."

His face turned a bright, unyielding shade of red. He was embarrassed. I was ashamed. Suddenly, I realized that I was the only one fighting this battle, the only one who knew it even existed. I locked myself in the bedroom for the rest of the night, trying to escape the firestorm I had created. Not only had I broken the no-fighting rule, I had embarrassed my husband over something as ridiculously stupid and trivial as a table. Plus, my son probably thought I was a maniac. *Who gets that upset over a table and homemade brownies?* I spent the next twenty-four hours hoping and praying that my husband would miraculously suffer a very friendly case of temporary amnesia. Otherwise, I had some major groveling to do.

The next evening I came home to the inviting scent of a delectable dinner consisting of perfectly cooked roast beef and fresh vegetables. The surprises continued when I found the dining room table set with our best china, an impressive bottle of wine, and an air of forgiveness. Apparently, my prayers had been answered.

"What's this?" I cautiously asked

"Your tone is a little different than last night," he replied.

"I'm sorry, that was ridiculous. I never should have said that about the tables. They are a good thing. They make everything so much easier."

"No, they make *dinner* so much easier. I guess I got a little carried away with them."

My heart melted. We were both right, and we were both wrong. It was undeniable—the tides had turned, and our relationship would never be the same again. Although it took me a little while to fully comprehend the meaning of agreeable, thanks to my husband's kindness, I eventually found my way. In contrast, he learned that no one likes feeling like they're married to their grandparent.

We now enjoy most of our dinners at the kitchen table, and my husband has thankfully embraced his real age. However, I'm not averse to breaking out the TV trays when our schedule demands a little compromise. On those nights, I make it a point to wait a little before returning the tables to their closet. I guess my husband was onto something because they're perfect for playing card games or sorting coupons. Just don't tell him I said that.

JENNY HILLS IS A WIFE AND MOTHER JUGGLING A CAREER AND blissful domesticity. When not writing, Jenny can be found watching *I Love Lucy*, dancing with her son, or cooking up a storm à la Julia Child. She loathes vacuuming, laundry, and bad casseroles. She is passionate about being a mama and loving her family. Jenny chronicles her attempts at balancing home, work, and the pursuit of happiness at her blog, Express Bus Mama.

The Corner Hutch Battle

By Susan A. Black

"NINETY DOLLARS," THE AUCTIONEER SAID. "SOLD TO THE woman in the blue coat; number twenty-eight."

The auctioneer slammed his gravel on a wooden block. He pointed it toward the ring man. The worker removed the lot number attached to the pinewood corner hutch and handed it to the clerk. She scribbled something in a ledger book and handed him a slip of paper. The young man bounded up the stairs and handed me the invoice. I beamed with pride at having secured my first auction item for our home.

At the opposite end of the sixty-acre property, my husband, Allen, was arranging for three of our steers to be marked for sale.

Three years earlier, we had moved from a small town in central Alberta to a hobby farm in the hamlet of Millet. My outdoor chore was to tend to the chickens. I cleaned their coop, set down clean straw in their nests, collected the eggs, and helped slay them. My mother-in-law had taught me how to chop off the hen's head, plunge the carcass into a large container of steaming hot water, and after a brief soaking, pluck its feathers.

By the time the ordeal was over, I was left with a good supply of frying chickens. It was our small herd of Charolais steers that gave me the most trouble. Once a week, I'd pack my newborn in a front carrier and clean out the chicken hut. The steers got excited by the smell of the soiled hay stacked just outside the building's narrow door and would stand in it, blocking my only way out. All my hollering didn't convince the invaders to back away. I was nervous and scared because all seven of the beasts were approaching the chicken coop. I lifted my shovel and slammed it on the broad forehead of the leading creature. It must have been in shock because it backed away and started kicking its hind legs. I tossed my weapon down and bolted to the gate, swung it open, and slipped my son and I through it. I pushed the lock into place and ran to the house. Later that evening, I shared my horror story with my husband.

"You're gonna get the steer all riled up. This breed is already skittish, so you better stay away from them."

"So, how do I get my eggs?"

"You can come with me in the morning, and I'll put them in the barn while you get the eggs."

My husband was a problem-solver and a hard worker. He had been a journeyman in the refrigeration and air conditioning industry. He also had an addiction to alcohol. My love for him was deep, but when he spent his evenings and weekends in an inebriated state, we didn't talk much. During the day, my husband drove into town for work.

I had left my job in the city. Our aim in those days was to develop our own company and expand ourselves as entrepreneurs. At first, I would travel with Allen to the nearby town, thirteen kilometers down a dirt road with our newborn strapped safely in his car seat. We had set up a small office, and my duties included answering the phone and taking work requests, invoicing the customers, and following up with banking. Within a year and a half, it became difficult to gather more business clients, and soon we had to give up the office space and work from our home. My husband spent the day in town waiting for me to send him on a client call. Perhaps the boredom caused him to visit the tavern and spend most of his days there. Eventually, the work orders ended.

To help support our life on the farm, we sold one of our vehicles to purchase cattle. Our idea was to raise, breed, and sell them.

"I'm going to the auction today to sell three steers," Allen said.

"I've never been to an auction. I'd like to go with you."

"We don't have any money for you to buy stuff, you know."

"I know we don't, but won't we make some on the Charolais?"

"We're not spending any of that money. We need it for feed."

"All of it? You mean we need to spend it all on those god-forsaken cows!"

"Steers," Allen said.

"We spend all our money on this dilapidated farm. I would like to have at least one piece of furniture in the house that is ours and not borrowed from your family."

"Do you hear yourself? We have a roof over our heads, a vegetable garden out front, a truck, and best of all, we've got our son."

"Yes, I know we have all that, but I still need to buy something at the auction."

"You don't mean that you need something, you mean that you want something."

"Don't tell me what I want or need. I need a break from you, that's what I really need."

I stomped to the bedroom and removed our precious bundle from his resting place. I could feel Allen's eyes staring at me as I prepared our baby for the journey to the auction site.

Afterward, I plunged my hand into the glass jar hidden in the back of the refrigerator and scooped out a roll of paper bills and a fistful of coins. I estimated there to be ninety dollars. As I slipped into my jacket, I heard the roar of the truck motor—our cattle transporter. I slung the diaper bag with its essential contents over my shoulder and headed out the door. We did not speak for the sixty-kilometer drive. I arrived at our destination still clinging to my childish mindset.

"I'm going to the stockade. Do you want to come along?" Allen said.

"I hate the smell of cattle. No thanks."

I turned around and walked to the auction house. I heard the auctioneer making a sale, drew the scent of roasting hotdogs into my nostrils, and felt a strong urge to find a seat in the bleachers. I settled in among the buyers and plucked my breast from its cover to feed my baby. I glanced at the paddle next to me and asked the man nearby about its meaning.

"If you're interested in buying something, hold it up and the auctioneer will see it."

When I spotted the corner hutch, I could not resist participating in the bidding war. It started at fifty dollars. I swung my paddle into action. The price raced to eighty dollars within a few minutes. Someone out of my sight was competing with me. I swung my paddle into the air.

The auctioneer eyed my bid and claimed it as the last.

Later, Allen arrived with two hotdogs and a frown.

"Honey, I lost the bid for that beautiful pinewood corner hutch. Do you see it; the one in the back?"

"Oh! You were bidding on that?"

"Yeah, I thought about what you'd said and thought you might like to have it. I got paid for the steers but only wanted to spend eighty dollars on it."

I handed him my payment slip and told him that I was his archrival. He cupped my face in his large hands and kissed my lips.

We loaded our wrapped treasure into the back of our empty truck and joked all the way home about our bidding battle. The corner hutch has since become a kind reminder of my deceased husband. I have passed it along to my son along with its tale.

SUSAN BLACK IS A PUBLISHED AUTHOR AND AN EXPLORER. HER travels overseas as an English teacher had her investigating life in various parts of China and several cities in Nepal, spending a few months in Bolivia, and enjoying a three-week seaside vacation in India. All the while, she continues to pursue her career as a writer. Her love of the written word begins with pencil and paper. She records her ideas in storyboard fashion and coverts ideas into prose. She has created three blog sites, so far, to compliment her many interests, including I Like That, The Little Red Book, and Ural Buddies. She currently resides in Campbell River, British Columbia, Canada, with her husband, Frank.

Same-Page Marriage Woes

By Marcia Kester Doyle

ANYONE WHO HAS BEEN MARRIED FOR ANY LENGTH OF time has had their share of disagreements. I've been married for thirty years, which qualifies me as a professional "argument" arbitrator. Some of the feuds I've had with my husband have been more serious than others, but you have to know when to pick your battles to get on equal footing.

The two of us come from very different backgrounds, each with our own set of emotional baggage. For the most part, we're on the same page, especially when it comes to parenting. But there are other issues in our marriage that have reduced us to foot-stomping, sulking toddlers when neither one of us is willing to give in. The issues we argue over most include:

Children. We want the best for our offspring, but sometimes we disagree about their choices. I have no problem with my children dating at the age of sixteen, but my husband would rather they wear a chastity belt until they're thirty-five. **Money.** This is the one subject that consistently pops up in our disagreements, because there is never enough of it to cover our expenses. My husband would love to drop some bills on a new bicycle, while I'm out scouting deluxe critter-condos for my five chinchillas. And neither one of us wants to fork over five-hundred dollars for a new water heater. Sudsing up in the oscillating lawn sprinkler just might be worth saving a few bucks. **Sex.** My spouse is a morning person, and I'm a night owl. I prefer to hide my imperfections by candle light. He, on the other hand, rises with the sun and is as chipper as a toddler cracked out on Coco Puffs cereal. **Friends.** Everyone has a friend that their spouse doesn't like. My husband has belligerent buddies who get drunk during sporting events and embarrass me with their rude comments. I have gal pals who love to chat it up all night over a bottle (or three) of wine. My husband refers to them as "yappers" who need to be muzzled after midnight. **Pets.** My spouse would be happy if there were no pets in our house. The little accidents on the carpet and the hairballs rolling around the floor like tumble weeds drive him to distraction. He feels that raising children is enough of a responsibility without adding critters to the mix. The night

I brought home a stray bunny to add to my growing zoo population, my husband threatened to make rabbit stew. We argued for days, but he finally relented because the nibbling critter keeps his mustache hairs neatly trimmed.

Time management. After financial issues, this is the second biggest issue on which we don't see eye to eye. When the kids were toddlers, we argued over whose turn it was to stay home and change diapers while the other person had free time with their friends. Now that we're older, free time is not an issue, since the adult kids have left the nest (and thankfully no one is still in diapers). The problem we face is trying to coordinate our schedules for family gatherings. Between strip bingo and pancake breakfasts at the Elk's Lodge, we rarely have time to schedule our colonoscopies together.

Technology. I was like a bear coming out of hibernation when it came to technology. I was the last one to own a cell phone, Kindle, or laptop. My husband brought me into the twenty-first century with my first iPod, which I had no clue how to use. When he tried to teach me the basic steps, I became frustrated and impatient. I couldn't grasp how something so small could be so complicated. The Hubs made the mistake of asking if I was born during the Jurassic period when I couldn't figure out how to use this wondrous gadget. The conversation ended when I chucked it at his beer belly.

Chores. The biggest question of the week in our house is: *Whose turn is it to clean the bathroom?* No one wants to scrub that toxic dump without a pressure cleaner and heavy-duty gloves. The kitchen isn't much better, since it looks like a bacon grease bomb has been detonated. We usually flip a coin to settle the argument. The Hubs still hasn't figured out why I always call "heads." (It's a two-headed coin.)

In-Laws. When you exchange weddings vows, you inherit more than a spouse. You inherit their crazy-ass relatives as well. It's like Forrest Gump's analogy of a box of chocolates: some might be nutty, and some might be rotten. And some might be deceptively hollow inside. The best compromise is to move a continent away from anyone else who shares your DNA.

Jealousy. When we're at parties and I see my husband flirting with a bleached blonde or a buxom brunette, my temper rises. I become like Medusa, my eyes zeroing in on him, willing him to turn to stone. If necessary, I bring out the big guns and publicly share that little tidbit about his painful hemorrhoids.

Marriage is never easy; it's a give-and-take relationship that needs to be nurtured in order to bloom. Trust, communication, and respect are the keys to a healthy marriage. After being together for thirty years, my husband and I have learned not to sweat the small stuff. In over words, there's no point in arguing over whose turn it is to change the grandchild's blow-out diaper. Pretty soon, we'll be changing each other's adult-size ones.

MARCIA KESTER DOYLE IS A NATIVE FLORIDIAN, MARRIED, AND the mother of four children. She is the author of the humorous blog, Menopausal Mother, where she muses on the good, the bad, and the ugly side of midlife mayhem. Bring her a jar of Nutella and some wine, and she'll be your best friend. Marcia is a contributing writer to Humor Outcasts, The Huffington Post, and What The Flicka?. Her work has also appeared on Scary Mommy, BlogHer, In the Powder Room, The Erma Bombeck Writers' Workshop, Mamapedia, Lost in Suburbia, Better after 50, Midlife Boulevard, Aiming Low, Generation Fabulous, Bloggy Moms, The Woven Tale Press, and numerous online communities. She is a BlogHer 2014 Voice of the Year and recently won VoiceBoks' Top Hilariously Funny Parent Blog 2014. Marcia was also voted into the Top 25 in the Circle of Mom's Funny Mom Blogs 2013. She is a contributing author to several books including: *The Mother of All Meltdowns, Sunshine After the Storm, Motherhood: May Cause Drowsiness, Parenting Gag Reel,* and *To Bliss and Back.* Her book, *Who Stole My Spandex?,* will be released in the fall of 2014.

And the Boob Wins

By R.C. Liley

T HIS ISN'T ABOUT AN ARGUMENT I'VE HAD WITH MY wife. This is about the battle with the boob—which wins, every damn time. We knew before we had a kid that when the day finally rolled around, I would become a stay-at-home dad. We were both working for a major financial company in the same office, and we both have degrees in finance. When we were both attending the same college (Boomer Sooner!), I thought finance was my true passion. Wrong. I started to get into fitness and nutrition and still am to this day.

The office environment became a major drag, as I couldn't stand being sedentary and surrounded by people who didn't care as much about their health. Work actually stressed me out so much that it was affecting me physically and had several doctors stumped on how to treat my condition.

On top of that, we never go out to eat, and since I'm the cook of the house, I spend a lot of time in the kitchen. I would go on a cooking marathon every weekend to ensure my wife and I had meals throughout the following week. I enjoyed providing healthy meals, but it meant less quality time spent together and even more stress as a result.

How would we manage all of this when we finally became parents? This question was asked a lot, which led to our unanimous decision that I would stay home with our future baby. Besides, we didn't need the added physical and emotional stress we'd face if we both kept our jobs—the expense of childcare alone is outrageous! The majority of my annual income would be spent on someone else taking care of my kid for at least eight hours a day during the week and most likely with other kids to manage as well. It just wasn't worth it.

I don't know how so many parents are able to wake up extra early to get their kids and themselves ready each day, and I don't want to know. With me staying at home to take care of our child and having more time to prepare meals, we would all have more quality time to spend with each other. That was our final decision.

Our precious daughter was born, and after my wife's extended maternity leave, I left the work force and started my life as an at-home dad. Fear, excitement, and confusion were the main emotions I had going into it, and after six months, they are still present every day. It turns out these feelings are common for any parent, and I don't expect they will go away anytime soon.

But these feelings, unlike how I felt going to work every day, are manageable and far more rewarding. I'm DAD, not employee number xyz filing in through the automatic doors of anguish. Now the only automatic doors I face are those at certain grocery stores when I make the weekly trip with my daughter. What's more, all of my symptoms of stress have disappeared as a result of me staying home, and I feel like a completely different person.

As far as our views on health and how to approach it with our daughter, my wife and I are on the same page. But this isn't true with everything. As a dad acting as full-time caregiver, my style of raising our child differs from how she would handle certain situations, like feeding.

My wife is awesome and selflessly ensures our daughter only receives the best nutrition with breast milk. Formula was never an option for us, and only now, at six months, are we introducing solids. I understand not all babies are able to enjoy an exclusive diet of breast milk, and we are incredibly happy that Avery is able and willing to accept the best nutrition from nature. As long as there are no issues, my wife will breastfeed our daughter for up to a year.

What I'm getting at is that I am dependent on the boob to provide me with bottles each day, so that I can feed our baby. The problem is that our daughter obviously prefers the fresh stuff, and although she'll accept the bottle (sometimes), it's never an easy feat. To say this is aggravating is an understatement; it gets under my skin and turns my face red with disappointment—not so much because I'm mad, but because I feel like I'm failing.

Sometimes I become so intent on providing for our daughter that my wife and I argue over how I approach feeding her. When we wake up in the morning, my wife has to get ready for work, so I start the first bottle of the day. The bottle fight ensues shortly thereafter, with various levels of resistance.

I'll admit, I do try to get her to take the bottle longer than I should, which adds to her fussiness. My dear wife lectured me on this (a lot), and now I'm more accepting when our baby won't take the bottle. I just give it a rest. If she continues to be fussy—maybe because she's really hungry now, and I'm not offering her a bottle—my wife gets on to me, thinking I'm trying to force her to eat. But that's not it. She's just fussy *and* hungry. You know, the typical baby!

Then my wife says that she'll feed her directly from the source and gets ready to unleash the two forces I can never compete with. Knowing she needs to get ready for work, we go back and forth arguing over who's going to feed our daughter breast milk. Eventually, after we waste time bickering, my wife heads to work, and I try offering the bottle again.

And, wouldn't you know, our baby surprisingly becomes accepting of the bottle when mom isn't around! I'm pretty confident that when mom is home, she knows she can have better than what's in the plastic beverage holder with a fake rubber nipple. She wants the real thing. So in a head-to-head competition, the boob wins against the bottle hands down, but the bottle is also very necessary for us guys.

As a stay-at-home dad, I'm useless if I'm not armed with bottles to feed our baby, and I depend on the boob to reload those bottles every day. I have now learned to listen better to my boob-wielding wife as she is still mom, and mom knows best when it comes to reading our baby's signals. Must be a womb thing.

At one point, I even made a list of the pros and cons of the bottle versus the boob. The boob still won:

Bottle Pros

Convenient and portable

Allows others to feed (gives mom a break)

Bottle Cons

Gets the healthy fat stuck on the side

Has to be cleaned afterward

Costs money

Not a boob

Boob Pros

Convenient and portable

Nothing to clean once done feeding

Free source of the best stuff

No fat stuck on the side

Boob Cons

Dad (or anyone else) can't use to feed baby

Babies eventually get teeth

I might regret saying it now, but I'll be thankful when our daughter grows past the breast milk phase and is strictly eating solid foods. Then I get to show her the marvelous world of food that we can experience together. Yes, stay-at-home parenting is a no-brainer to us, as it enables our child to never be without a parent. I couldn't imagine the thought of another person or a facility watching over my daughter while I sit in an office desperately wanting to get out and see my kid. When someone asks what I do, I'm proud to declare that I'm a stay-at-home dad raising my beautiful girl. I may not earn an income in a monetary sense, but her smiles pay me in ways money never could. It's rewarding, even when the boob wins.

R.C. LILEY SHARES THE INS AND OUTS OF HIS NEW LIFE AS A STAY-at-home dad raising his daughter, Avery, on his blog, Going Dad. He's a health-conscious parent on a mission to keep healthy and live green.

By Jessica Azar

Fishing for a Break, Not Sea Bass

By Jessica Azar

THE ENTIRE "EPISODE" WAS SET INTO MOTION BY MY husband's invitation to go on a multiple-day, deep-sea fishing trip with some guys from work. A vendor for his company was paying for the trip, and he loves to fish, so naturally he was dying to go. I don't begrudge my sweet husband the chance to relax and get away from the madness of our daily lives, but when he does, I'm left holding the bag—and this bag contains our four sweet, but wild children, and their crazy schedules, alone. It never fails that whenever my husband goes out of town, whacktacular things happen at our house. I do my best to take things in stride, but I still feel like I'm barely staying afloat—and that's on my good days.

I had successfully prayed the trip into being cancelled and rescheduled two times, but the third time I was un-

203

successful. So I started pulling out the big guns, like guilt. "This is one of the worst weeks for you to go!" I whined.

He gave me an irritated look and said, "Jessica, I'm going. This week won't be as bad as next week when all of the 'end of the year' activities and stuff begin."

I refused to let this go. "But I'll be so tired and stressed from this week of handling them all alone that next week will be even worse!" I huffed.

With an exasperated edge, he said, "You'll be FINE."

I harrumphed and turned to deal with our youngest daughter, who wanted to be picked up and was throwing a fit. This was not going the way I wanted it to go. But I had other matters to handle, and I started to convince myself that things would be okay. We'd have fun doing things that their daddy doesn't like to do. I'd have plenty of time to myself to write and watch my shows on TV at night.

I was starting to get past the being mad phase and progressing to mildly irritated when he informed me that he would be playing softball the night before his departure. "Doing WHAT?" I sputtered. "You're already going to be gone for most of the week! Can't you back out?"

Not only was I unhappy about him not being available to help with the kids, I was also dismayed that I would have to be away from him that much longer. Even after being married for nine years and together as a couple for twelve, I still can't get enough of him. He should be honored.

"No, Jessica, I can't back out. I made a commitment to them. Plus, I'm the pitcher," said the High Roller. I swear

I saw his chest puff out a bit as he said it. Men and their games.

"FINE!" I yelled, and stalked off to see which kid was screaming about what—because there's always a screaming kid around here. I gave him the cold shoulder when he left town the next morning. He tried to be sweet about it, but I intended to make my point. I only gave him one kiss before he left. Yep. I was vicious.

After a rough and tiring, but normal, Tuesday of him being gone, I was looking forward to Wednesday, which is my most relaxing day of the week. I only have one child out of four from 9:00 a.m. until 2:00 p.m.—and that's the one who naps with me for a couple of hours during that time! In that short window, I'm able to get household chores finished that are otherwise nearly impossible—or even (*gasp*) write in peace! Undisturbed! What a concept!

To stress the importance of this specific Wednesday: it was the last Wednesday with this schedule until fall. School was nearing an end, and the following Wednesday both of the middle kids would have their class parties in the morning. This was my last Wednesday of semi-solitude and freedom before the deluge of summer insanity. Except it was not meant to be.

At wake-up time on Wednesday morning, my seven-year-old son, whom I'll call Butch Cassidy, started complaining that his ear was killing him. He never complains about physical pain, so I knew it had to be bad. Although I was already mentally grumbling, I decided that I would take all four kids with me to Urgent Care when it opened at 8:00 a.m. and then take Sundance, my six-year-old son, and the Princess, my four-year-old daughter, to school when it opened at 9:00 a.m. Then, if the doctor said he wasn't contagious, I'd take Butch Cassidy to his school.

I thought I'd concocted the perfect plan. Boy, was I wrong. I loaded the entire herd into the car and drove to our destination, only to find no cars in the Urgent Care parking lot. None—as in the doctors, nurses, and staff hadn't been there before opening time preparing for the day.

Sundance said, "Mama! Look at all of the signs on the door! They say CLOSED. We're doomed."

I mentally agreed with him as I pulled up to take a closer look. Apparently, this was the one day out of the whole freaking year that they were closed for scheduled maintenance—whatever that means. It was like a website that had gone offline. A real-life 404. *What were the odds?* Mine weren't looking good.

I quickly realized (as my son incessantly complained about his ear pain from the backseat) that I would have to attempt to get an appointment with the pediatrician. *Gulp.* I loathe the pediatrician's office. I love my kids' doctor, but hate the germy, Lord of the Flies-esque waiting room full of loud, rambunctious kids. And it always takes forever to get seen, unless you have the first appointment of the day. One can only obtain this mythical golden ticket of appointments by being the first-answered caller at 8:00

a.m. I began feverishly dialing, hanging up, and redialing when the busy signal alerted me that I was not first in line. It's like calling in on a radio station's "Be the ninth caller!" giveaway contest, except this time I was competing for a damn doctor's appointment instead of tickets.

The receptionist finally answered. An appointment was available at 9:00 a.m. with one of the doctors we like. I breathed a sigh of relief. But what was I supposed to do with everyone until appointment time? It was an hour until I could drop the middle two kids off, and I had no cash to pay for them to go to Early Day. A boulder of dread hit my stomach at the prospect of having to haul all of the kids to the doctor's office. I made a snap decision to go to the bank and pull some cash from the ATM, which I very rarely do. We drove over to the bank, and—the parking lot was torn up for maintenance!

I couldn't drive up to the ATM. The parking lot was completely blocked off from vehicles. I was so desperate that I figured, "Heck, I'll park the car and jump through the bushes to the ATM." My hopes were quickly shot down, when an "Out of Order" sign greeted me. Seriously? SERI-OUSLY? I started laughing the laugh of a sleep-deprived mom coming unglued and drove to another bank down the street. *Guess what?* Their ATM was out of order too!

Stubbornness and sick curiosity drove me onward. I refused to give up, although I probably should've taken this as a sign to go home and hide under the bed. So I drove to yet another bank, successfully got twenty dollars out of the ATM, and paid a five-dollar fee without even caring. I then drove the middle kids to Early Day, dropped them off without incident, and headed to the doctor with the ailing Butch Cassidy and LLL, my wild, two-year-old daughter.

We arrived at the doctor's office. When I went to take LLL out of her seat, a nauseating odor hit me in the face. *Nooo*, I begged internally, knowing full well that she had a nasty diaper blowout. I changed her, cleaned up her seat the best I could, left the windows cracked to air the car out, and moved on. I carried her into the doctor wearing only her shirt and diaper. We walked in to the office and as I signed in, I was informed that the doctor we had made the appointment with had left for an emergency, so we would be lumped in with another doctor's schedule—my least favorite doctor. Most moms that I know avoid this type of doctor like the plague. She's condescending and rude and has the bedside manner of a drill sergeant. She's also slow as Christmas, and the fact that our appointment was being combined into her schedule meant things would be even more delayed. It was a pediatrician's office traffic jam.

I sighed and sat down to fill out the yearly update forms for my son. We sat in the outer waiting room for close to an hour. I did my best to keep LLL from licking the floor and harassing sick kids while Butch Cassidy kept trying to slide across the filthy, faded linoleum tile like Tom Cruise in *Risky Business*.

There must be something about the very air of the doctor's office that makes sick kids act like wild animals.

Finally, our name was called, and we went into the smaller holding cell (exam room). The nurse took his vitals, and then we waited awhile for the beloved doctor to come in. After I had entertained LLL with every book and puzzle I could find and tested Butch Cassidy on every math skill I could think of, she ambled in and diagnosed him with an ear infection. Now she is notoriously overly hesitant to write prescriptions, and, yes, I know that antibiotics have been over-prescribed, which is a bad thing. But please don't tell me we should "wait and see" if the full-blown ear infection you just diagnosed resolves itself. I don't have the time, the cash, or the sanity to bring him back again to reconfirm a freaking ear infection.

After I got squirrelly, she resentfully wrote the prescription, and we headed for the parking lot. LLL did NOT want to get back into the nasty smelling car seat she had fouled earlier, so I had to wrestle and bribe her into submission before driving to the pharmacy.

We bought the antibiotic and pain medicine, went home, and I dosed him up. In the process, I made a fatal mistake: I did not put the lid back on the top of the liquid antibiotic before setting it on the counter. LLL grabbed the bottle before I could stop her, and it went everywhere. It was a pink tidal wave filling every crack and crevice known to kitchen.

LLL licked it off of her now antibiotic-coated arms and looked like something akin to the movie *Carrie, Prom Night*—just substitute the pig's blood for this mess. Barely enough of the liquid was left for another dose, much less the prescribed ten days. At that point, I put them both down for a nap, because I was at the end of my rope. Then I realized it was time to go pick up the middle two kids from preschool.

I have so many things to be thankful for, but this day was not one of them. Some days just suck. My husband owes me big time, and I may never be okay with him going away again.

JESSICA MCNEILL AZAR, AUTHOR OF THE POPULAR blog, Herd-Management.com, is a happily married stay-at-home mom to four kids ages seven, six, four, and two. She holds a Bachelor of Arts in English with a Minor in Writing from Auburn University Montgomery, is a Huffington Post contributing blogger, and also writes for websites like Mamapedia, *Venn Magazine*, Scary Mommy, and BLUNTmoms. Her work appears in three humor anthologies. As a writer and Mental Health Advocate, Jessica is also co-authoring an anthology which will be called *Laughter is the Best Medicine; Using Humor to Survive Mental Illness.* She enjoys running and drinking single-malt Scotch in the evenings to soothe her kid-rattled nerves.

To Infinity and Beyond

By m.nicole.r.wildhood

IN 2006, I HAD A LAPSE OF JUDGMENT THAT LASTED JUST long enough to severely injure my otherwise healthy GPA: I declared a double degree in English and chemical engineering. I wanted to save the world, but I also loved to write; surely the answers to the looming energy crisis were buried somewhere in chemistry, for which I could hunt without giving up my poetry compulsion. It took a friend quipping, "Well, you could always use essays as an alternative source of fuel," to reveal (to me) the full futility of my grand plan.

I quit engineering, but not before failing Calc 2. It wasn't that I didn't understand; it was that I didn't agree. I attended four different math professors' office hours seeking an explanation for how an infinite number of numbers could be added to produce a finite sum. Eventually, it all came down to something like, "We do this because it works." In other words, just accept it and move on.

I did manage to move on at least. I moved out of state, finished college, and met a boy. All the while, I really hoped that, somehow, my several-semester foray into engineering would not be for naught. As it turned out, the boy I met had earned an engineering degree from a large state school like the one where I took calculus, and he was now working as a structural engineer in a fancy firm downtown. Over the rather rocky, five-year runway to our wedding, Mark remained consistently the consummate engineer. On walks around our beautiful *Northwet* city, Mark would mutter technical words under his breath when we passed under bridges. He would excitedly scramble over to the window if we were passing a construction site while riding the bus. On occasion, he would take personal offense if a substandard material was used in the construction of a building or bridge.

Eventually, I began to understand enough of his outbursts to ask questions and, once I started, I quickly discovered that my math classes would not go to waste! They would prove useful fodder for the fires of our fights. My inquiries about specific structures always led to debates about abstract math constructs—and a debate we've since between is whether Sir Isaac Newton discovered calculus or *invented* it. Other aspects of calculus were not so easily resolved:

"You cannot add up an infinite number of numbers and get a finite sum!" I would shout and wring my hands.

"But it *works*," Mark would say. "People have been doing it for a long time."

"But it contradicts itself! By mathematicians' own definition of infinite, you can't add something forever and end in a discrete place."

"I think you can if the numbers are infinitely small."

"But you still have an infinite number of them!"

"Right," Mark said, infuriatingly calm every time, "an infinite number of infinitely small numbers."

It would be about six months before anyone intervened in this seemingly infinite madness.

Mark's older brother holds a PhD in computer science and works for a big-name tech company. A father of three, he is a gentle, soft-spoken man with exactly the same voice as his younger brother. Being brothers, they love to play the surround-sound prank by sneaking up behind me and mumbling to each other. This obviously sounds like Mark muttering scatteredly to himself and unsettles me, much to their delight. In person, his intelligence shows up mostly in his humor. We presented our math dilemma to him earnestly over the phone (he lives a few states away), the details of the argument largely being recalled from my sticky memory punctuated by Mark's clarifications.

"So you see," I said as if preparing to bow, "an infinite number of numbers could not add up to a finite sum no matter how small each number is. That's just not what 'infinite' means."

I pause, and shoot a nervous look at Mark. His brother said, "Yes, I'm skeptical myself." A little balloon started filling triumphantly in my chest. Our erstwhile endless problems were over—until they weren't (which shouldn't have surprised me given the apparently flexible definition of infinite).

"Set theory," Mark recently began excitedly, "is a really weird thing. Technically, if you have an infinite set of infinities, the set itself is bigger than infinity. Isn't that totally strange?" Mark was nearly giddy.

"What's your point?" I asked, intrigued.

"Just that the definition of infinite isn't as rigid as we thought."

"Well, if that's true, then words have no meaning," I sighed.

Mark smiled. "It seems that our fight is about the definition of infinite now."

"Indeed," I could feel my engines revving up. "Or what constitutes a 'definition' at all." Mark looked bewildered.

"For instance," I said, "getting back to your set theory example, how can you possibly have more than one infinity and still be able to use the word 'infinite'?"

"Probably the best way to explain it is to think of each infinity in the set as represented by a different object. So, you know, one is an infinite number of cars, one is an infinite number of trees, one is an infinite number of houses."

By m.nicole.r.wildhood

"Well, that seems to be what everyone seems to think, anyway."

Mark seemed startled, and the fight lost a bit of steam. "Sure," he said, and then hesitated. "But they're just symbols to explain set theory." Another pause. "As much as it can be explained anyway. I mean, the idea of anything being bigger than infinity is just mind-boggling ... just like infinity itself is mind-boggling!"

"Mind-boggling indeed. Hence my point that you cannot add up an infinite number of numbers and get a finite sum."

"Because infinity is so big?" Mark was genuinely confused.

"Yes! It's so big that it never ends. As in, there is never a sum."

"Right," Mark said slowly, "when you're talking about big infinity." He studied my face. "Infinity, as it turns out, has to be defined further for it to be useful."

"But the definition of infinite is that it goes on forever. Therefore, adding something an infinite number of times means that you're adding something forever. It's just nonsensical to say that it will be a finite sum. You can't have both infinity and not infinity." I said, breathlessly, and a little embarrassed that I was so.

"Things can be infinitely big or infinitely small, though."

"What? That's basically saying that infinity can be different sizes."

"Precisely!" Mark smiled hopefully.

"No. See, as soon as you say different sizes of infinity, you're talking about something else. You're not talking about infinity."

"Well, that depends." Mark's voice started to get tight. "When you say, 'adding an infinite number of numbers can produce a finite sum if the numbers are infinitely small,' the thing that is infinitely big is the amount, or set, of numbers you're adding. The thing that is infinitely small is the size of each number."

"But the definition of 'infinite' ... that is, 'something that goes on forever' ... stays the same, it's the 'big' or 'small' that changes." I leaned back. Surely he would see the logic here.

He paused, about to concede the point, clearly. "That's exactly *my* point, though." Mark said carefully. "If the smallness of the numbers 'goes on forever,' then it wouldn't matter how many of them you had ... that is, the amount of them could go on forever ... you'd still get a finite sum."

"But why doesn't the *amount* of numbers trump the *size* of each?" Unbelievably, I was trying not to raise my voice. "The fact that you will never have an end of numbers, because there are infinitely many of them, kind of means by definition that you can't get a finite sum because infinite means 'goes on forever.'"

"Well," Mark started, but before he could finish, I threw my hands up.

"That's like saying 'purple things aren't purple.' Does the world mean nothing anymore?"

At this point, we both collapsed into giggles. Depending on your definition, this fight—whether it is big or small—could be infinite.

M.NICOLE.R.WILDHOOD IS A COLORADO NATIVE WHO HAS BEEN missing the sun since she moved to Seattle in 2006, but finds the staggering array of abundant plant life stunning and spiritually nourishing. She has been a saxophone player and registered scuba diver for over half her life, and enjoys long bike rides with her husband. She writes poetry and short nonfiction; her poems and essays have appeared in Christian poetry journals, regional contest anthologies, and on poetry blogs. After two years of dips into various majors at CU Boulder, she earned a BA in Christian Theology from Seattle Pacific University in 2010.

Dirty Socks, Everywhere

By Angela Keck

I T WAS THE MORNING OF MY DAUGHTER'S THIRD BIRTH-
day, her first birthday in our new home, which was finally
big enough to host our families. I was at once excited and
dreading the experience. Excited to see my little girl's face
when she spotted her Scooby-Doo birthday cake, excited
to watch her open presents, excited to show off our new
home to family members who hadn't seen it yet. *Dreading
showing off our home to family members who hadn't seen it yet.*

I should explain, *right?* Well, my in-laws are not your
average, run-of-the-mill folks—they're clean freaks. I don't
mean that in an unkind way, as I know "freak" can have a
bad connotation in some circles. What I mean, is that they
enjoy their home being as I envision a clean room might
be at Apple headquarters. They think everyone else should
keep their houses the same way, and doing otherwise is a
sign of laziness, or worse. I, on the other hand, want my

house to at least be less than filthy. Normally, I might ignore the clutter until I'm a little less exhausted—which is never—which means my house is perpetually cluttered.

For this event, I wanted the house to be picked up, dusted, and vacuumed within an inch of its life. So my sister came over that morning to help me clean. We had only lived in our house for a few months. There were still things that hadn't been put away or stored. There was also the usual clutter from three people and a dog living in a very small house.

But we had a plan! First we'd pick everything up, then we'd vacuum, then we'd dust, and then we'd be done. So we jumped right in with the general picking up.

We were so obliviously arrogant in our naiveté.

When I found the first pair of socks sitting next to my husband's recliner in the living room, I wasn't all that shocked. I was aware that he sat there every day when he got home from work, relaxing for a few minutes before ditching his shoes and socks. I've picked dirty socks up from there before.

On this day, there were at least three pairs scattered about in various stages of decomposition. I don't know about you, but my socks are not *crunchy* after I take them off. His are.

Ewww!

I was grossed out and a little bit annoyed. Seriously, he's a grown man. *Can he not pick up after himself?*

But, alas, I moved on.

Cleaning in the office, next to the computer desk, I found two more pairs of dirty socks.

Onto the bathroom. More dirty socks!

Quickly approaching a dozen pairs of dirty socks found in all corners and all spaces of the house, I can feel my eye starting to twitch. There were little black, scrunched-up balls of sweat and ick left strategically all around the house for me to pick up and deal with. To be fair, I hadn't yet found any in the laundry room.

The last room on the list to clean was the kitchen. And that's when I found them. I'd found dirty socks in a lot of places in our house in our five years of marriage. It was kind of a thing with us: he ditches dirty socks, and I complain about it. But this—this was taking it to new heights.

There before me a pair of socks sat chilling on the kitchen table.

That's right! Right there, amongst the junk mail and other clutter that had accumulated through the previous couple of days, was a pair of his hard, crusty, lifeless, ewwwy socks.

I looked at my sister, and she could see there was an eruption about to happen. She knew there was a meltdown coming, but my husband was still not home from work. I had several hours to stew and let the steam build before I could release it on him.

Through the rest of the afternoon, I kept mumbling to myself as the volcano stirred inside of me. Then I heard what I had been waiting for all day: the sound of his car in the driveway and the gate opening as he came home from work. I grabbed every single one of those dirty socks and met him at the back door.

"Hi, honey—" He didn't have a chance to finish his greeting. He saw my face, and he saw my fists full of dirty socks and knew all hell was about to break loose. He might be occasionally lazy with his laundry, but he's no dummy.

"I want you to know," I said, "that I've spent the entire day cleaning this house so that we can have our families over to celebrate our daughter's birthday and that I have found at least one pair of your dirty socks in every single room!" I held the socks up as evidence that I wasn't exaggerating (except for not mentioning the sock-free laundry room).

This is when he made his fatal error in judgment.

He started to laugh.

As any sane man will tell you, when confronted with a crazy wife who is mid-meltdown, the last thing you want to do is anger her more by laughing. It's kind of like poking an angry bear with a sharp stick. It makes the bear mad and dramatically shortens your life span!

"Don't you dare laugh at me, and you had better listen to me very carefully. If I ever find another pair of your dirty socks in any location other than inside the effing laundry hamper, you will be walking funny for a very long time!"

"I'm sure you didn't really find those in every room," he piped up.

"EVERY SINGLE ROOM!" I fired back.

"Not the kitchen." He sounded so victorious as he trumpeted that to me that I probably enjoyed this last part a little too much.

"Yes, even the kitchen! And not just in the kitchen, but in the middle of the table! Dirty socks on my kitchen table! MY TABLE! I mean honestly, what the hell?"

"Technically, it's OUR table. And those were clean!"

I'm sure he believed that statement when he said it. He insisted that he had gone to put on a pair of socks while sitting at the table and then forgot to put them on, so they were clean. I can say with certainty that clean does not resemble a dried-up old potato.

We recently celebrated our twentieth wedding anniversary, and I'm happy to tell you that I have never had to pick up another pair of his socks since that day.

And he doesn't walk funny either.

ANGELA KECK IS THE AUTHOR BEHIND, WRITER MOM'S BLOG. SHE is also a featured contributor on The Huffington Post, What The Flicka?, Mamapedia, Scary Mommy, Mamalode, and many other sites. She loves writing about anything that moves her or makes her smile. Blogging allows her to combine her day job as an online community and social media professional with her love of writing. Angela lives in Southern Illinois with her husband of twenty years, her two children, one German Shepherd, and one extremely fat cat.

The Boyfriend Fallacy

By Alexa Bigwarfe

FOR TWO LONG DAYS, CRAMMED INTO THE CAB OF A pickup truck, we drove in mostly complete silence. From Columbia, South Carolina all the way to San Angelo, Texas—more than twelve hundred miles. Every once in a while, I'd get a dirty look shot in my direction or a grunt when I gave him directions or asked him questions related to our trip. But beyond that, there was minimal interaction. It was torture. Talk about a mindfuck. Especially since I didn't even know what had happened. But I had already learned this fact about JD—until he's ready to talk about something, the silent treatment and some occasional death stares were the best I was going to get.

So we drove. Through South Carolina, Georgia, Alabama, and Mississippi, where we finally stopped for the night at a dump of a motel. After a restless night, in which I continually jumped up to peek into the parking lot to make sure no one was stealing my belongings out of the back of the truck, we got up, still without talking to each other, and started on day two of the trip.

Onward across the rest of Mississippi, Louisiana, and into Texas. And on, and on, and on through Texas. We had driven a thousand miles without speaking a word. It was early July. I was hot and beginning to get a little crabby.

I tried to pretend that everything was fine, which probably only heightened his level of annoyance with me. I sang along to the music, flipped through some magazines, and tried to take in some of the scenery—until it was absolutely driving me crazy. *Why? Why was he so pissed off at me? What was this argument even about?* I replayed every tiny detail of the moment leading up to his explosion and could not put together anything that made sense.

I know that the situation had been chaotic. I had a lot of crap that we were trying to fit into a small U-Haul trailer and the back of our pickup truck to haul to my new home—for at least the next year—at Goodfellow Air Force Base.

What events had happened that elevated our usual sniping at each other to this state?

I could only think of two possible explanations:

The tarp. We were dealing with an uncooperative tarp that did not want to cover my belongings. Moving is stressful. No doubt. The stupid tarp came undone about five minutes down the highway and began flapping around. So we pulled over and re-secured it.

Annoying? Yep. But this certainly couldn't be the culprit of all this vitriol, could it?

It had to be something else.

The phone call. While we were in the midst of trying to cram all of my crap in the truck and get the stupid tarp tied down, the phone rang. My mother handed it over to me. It was some stupid survey that, for some reason, in my momentary lapse of judgment, I decided to answer.

I could see the steam starting to pour from JD's eyes and ears as I answered the surveyor's questions.

"Just hang up!" he seethed.

Annoying? Sure. I had left him to deal with the tarp while I took an unnecessary phone call. Enough to merit the poison-dart glares? I didn't think so. Certainly, he could not be this mad at me over a stupid phone call and an unpredictable tarp.

I replayed the two events in my mind, trying to make sense of the situation. Finally, I turned to question him, but as soon as I started to say something, his nonverbal response spoke quite loudly. He was not ready to talk to me.

The cat, however, wouldn't stop talking. He was not a fan of being trapped in the car either. But at least I had some sort of interaction as we covered miles and miles of Nowhere America.

After the first day, I was getting quite annoyed. This could've been a fun road trip. We only had one week together before he had to return to his duty station in North

Carolina, and I'd be in Texas for eight to twelve months. Why was he wasting our precious time together being mad at me? Over what?

Once again, I replayed the events of the morning before we left my mother's house and headed on our way. Hectic packing and loading, the annoying survey call—and oh yeah, my mom and I looked at a map of Texas to see how far Corpus Christi was out of the way. I thought it would be nice to stop there for a day or two at the beach if it wasn't a ridiculous detour. Turns out, it was quite off the path, so I scrapped that idea. We would just head to San Angelo.

So why, *why for the love of all things holy*, was JD so freaking mad at me?

Finally, midway through day two, I determined I *would* get an answer.

Despite the clear warning signs of danger, I forced him to talk to me. Besides, where else could he go? We were trapped on a single bench seat inside our two-door GMC Sierra pickup truck, in the middle of No Man's Land, Texas.

He told me that he couldn't believe I had taken a phone call—a stupid phone call—in the middle of trying to get packed and ready to go, leaving him to do all the work.

I kept prodding. I knew there had to be more. That was way too insignificant to merit this backlash.

Finally, it came spewing out.

"I cannot believe you would look at a map *right in front of me* to determine how you could go visit your little boyfriend after I leave."

My head snapped in his direction so fast, I thought it might spin right off.

"WHAT?"

"I saw you and your mom trying to figure out how far it was to Corpus Christi."

"Seriously? What boyfriend?" I was dumbfounded.

"You know ... that guy from Officer Training School in Texas who said he has a sailboat and would teach you how to sail."

Once I figured out who he was even referring to, I started laughing out loud. JD did not find anything funny.

"First of all, I barely know that guy. Second of all, he's from San Antonio, which is nowhere near Corpus Christi. And third of all, I was *trying* to plan a little getaway for us to the beach, you moron."

I kept chuckling. He was jealous. That was kind of cute. However, I did not find it funny that he would rather completely shut me out and treat me like crap for two days rather than talk to me about the situation. We could have saved so much time if he'd just *asked* me why I was looking up the route to the beach rather than *assuming* I was planning a secret rendezvous with a guy I barely knew.

"Furthermore," I continued, "I had already forgotten he even mentioned sailing to me, so why on earth do *you* remember that little conversation?"

He didn't have to answer. I got it. We were both in the military. We would be stationed thousands of miles apart. I would be alone with all kinds of single, young airmen. He was worried. If he had internalized that one little comment, I knew the separation would be difficult for us.

But I still had to laugh. I could not believe he'd been so angry at me. Well, once I learned the real cause of his anger, I did understand, but I still giggled when I thought about the situation.

As it turned out, the next few years were really crazy for us. I had been stationed at Goodfellow AFB for about three months when September 11, 2001 happened. Over the next few years, both of us were deployed numerous times, but we stayed together. We had to learn to trust each other and trust our love. I had to learn *not* to mention to JD any insignificant comments or suggestions from men I became friends with in the service. And I did my best to ensure that whenever JD visited, he spent time with my friends so that he felt comfortable with the men and women I spent so much time with. While it was a ridiculous argument, it taught me a great deal about our communications styles and our relationship.

Eventually, in 2003, when we were both in the United States at the same time, we were able to get married.

All these years later, I still give him a hard time about visiting my boyfriend in Corpus Christi—and how ridiculous he was for jumping to that conclusion. Thankfully, we can now both laugh about it.

ALEXA BIGWARFE IS A FREELANCE WRITER AND AUTHOR. SHE recently edited and published a book for grieving mothers entitled *Sunshine After the Storm: A Survival Guide for the Grieving Mother* and has been published in two anthologies, *The Mother of All Meltdowns* and *The HerStories Project*. She is currently co-authoring a book entitled *Lose the Cape: Realities from Busy Modern Moms and Strategies to Survive*, due out in spring 2015. She launched her writing with the blog No Holding Back, as an outlet for her grief after the loss of one of her twin daughters to Twin to Twin Transfusion Syndrome (TTTS). Alexa is a wife, mother of three, dog owner, advocate, and sometimes political activist.

A Record of a Fight

By Brian Sorrell

(Inspired by Mark Twain's *Journalism in Tennessee*)

I FELT MYSELF BOILING OVER AS I PICTURED HOW THE fight I was about to start would go:

I took the last slug of whiskey from the bottle, smashed it over the counter next to the sink, and stormed into the living room armed with the jagged bottle neck, kicking shards of shattered glass ahead of me, the last drops of liquor dripping onto my leather boots. Out of my mouth came the stink of fresh booze and a fucking goddamned strong desire to know who the fuck you think you are, while I'm off doing you a favor, and the one reason you'll get off that fucking couch is to fuck with me?

"What's your problem this time, Mister Short-Fuse?" she asked, while pulling out a switchblade and flicking it casually. In the light, it shone like a mirror in my eyes. I knew she was serious when she said, quite unfussed by my dramatic entrance, "That's no way to start a conversation."

We lunged at one another and missed. She carved a hole a foot long in my favorite side chair, and I knocked over her floor lamp, glass bottle neck smashing against the glass bulb. It scattered to the floor, crunching under my knees as I got back to my feet, bloodied, dripping red, and pooling in my shoes.

"Next time I step out of the room," I said, "you better remember I'll be stepping back in."

She deflected my swing, stopping my arm mid-punch with a spin kick that dislocated my elbow. On the way around, she picked up a dinner plate, with a couple of chicken bones left on it, and flung it at my throat the way she'd toss a Frisbee across the beach at a family picnic. The chicken bones stung me in the neck, but I ducked in time to dodge the plate. It smashed into a shelf of family pictures and busted the glass out of every one with me in it. Lucky toss.

I looked at her, and felt my eyes squint and my mouth snarl. "You're so fucking smart. Well, listen up, because I'm saying this once and for all. My choices matter too around here."

She looked at me like I was speaking Chinese and screamed so loud the trim paint on the door jamb started to peel. She paused and drew in a deeper breath, as if she'd just been warming up, and let out a belt that bent the steel of the door hinges. The kitchen door swung open and shut, fast and loud. You could hear a bird shriek its final tweet and die, falling out of the honey-locust tree in the front yard. Even the stray neighborhood cats scattered away from the scene.

"You're the one who didn't give a shit about that dated crap. Like you said ... you said it," she told me again and again. "I did what I did," she said, "and that's all there is."

I ignored her and tore down the ceiling light we'd put up last week to spruce up the room and bring a little cheer into the place. I ripped the wires out, stripped off some insulation with my teeth, and held the two ends in front of me. I spat between them, and a spark arced and glowed orange hot for an instant before exploding in a blue flash. I stuck the two ends across the stem of her favorite houseplant, and it wilted right before our eyes, giving up.

"That's how it feels," I told her, snarling and squinting still. "That's how it feels. You want to feel it too?"

She picked up the sleeper sofa and flipped the bed out as a shield, looking like lounge-suite riot gear. She fished a loose quarter out of the cracks, and didn't say a word when she pinch-flicked the coin toward my head. Ducking, it lodged in my ear canal and rang like an ambulance siren. I saw her mouth moving, but I couldn't hear a word—it looked like something about how much I fucking care what you want to hear every minute of the day you fussy son of a bitch.

About this time, a local film crew showed up. They started to set up a lighting rig since we'd busted out all the lights. I guess they'd heard the ruckus. You never know when you'll get just the right moment on camera and splash your name across social media and the six-o'clock news. Seems they were drunk on the possibility of virality, parched by their own vanity. By the sound of things outside, this battle was already turning out to be a doozy that the world would show on repeat. Best get it on film.

A couple of guys with handheld cameras on stabilizers took positions in the corners of the room, safely out of the way of the melee. The guy with the boom mic looked leery of the whole situation and tiptoed around the whiskey bottle and smashed-up picture frames. The director sat down uneasily in an empty club chair that our son usually sits in, but he was still asleep in the other room. The director said, "No I'll be alright. Just keep on going."

So we did.

My hearing was just about fading back in, when the downbeats of the wrong song on the turntable fired me back up. I grabbed the car keys from atop the fridge, hatching a new plan. I got my waffle-head framing hammer out of the top drawer and left a line of crisscross circles in the walls, warming up my swing to smash through the ranch slider to the veranda overlooking the driveway. I jumped through the glass hanging from the doorframe and bloodied up my hand pretty good as I leapt from the porch to the hood of the car. I rolled off the far side before she could douse me with a pan of hot chicken grease she'd just thrown from the kitchen window. The grease dripped down the front fender and onto the tire. The tire burst and a shotgun blast of rubber sprayed all over the front lawn, covering the corpse of that poor bird that fell dead out of the honey locust.

I clawed at the door handle and opened it, and crawled into the driver's seat using the door as a shield as she pelted the car with kitchen knives, cast-iron pots, and the motor base of the blender. She flung a pizza stone like it was a throwing star, and it sliced through the windshield. It knocked the rearview mirror onto my face and broke my nose. I ducked down under the steering column, blood all over the floor mats, and stuffed the key in the ignition. "I'll get her," I muttered as I cranked the engine. I hit the gas with my right hand and held the wheel with my left. I threw the goddamned thing into drive and hoped for the worst.

The wheels screeched and cut up the curb. Right over the grass, our little hatchback ripped through the porch and half under the house, taking out most of the living room floor. The coffee table I'd built some years back fell through and shattered against the roof of the car. I grabbed a splintered leg and swung it wildly, yelling something about poor choices.

The director looked down at me, furrowed his brow, and shook his head. "Really?" They quit filming.

At this point I realized how ridiculous I sounded.

Whenever I stop to think about it, I end in the same spot. Fights are all vanity. Why on earth would the woman I love, who loves me as much, want to hurt me? And worse—why would I feel the need to start and *win* an altercation with this angel? There ain't no scorecards at the end of the argumentative marriage floor routine. No judges. No audience cheering us on. And competing without scorecards is a sure sign of a vain nature.

It's always petty. It's always mountains out of molehills, as they say. Take our knock-down, drag-out episode here. It was simple really. Our four-year-old son was asleep in his room when our neighbor popped by for a visit and a beer. As we usually do, we set the records spinning, listening to tunes and talking about the old times. I picked one out and put it on. All I wanted to hear was the last track more than anything. So I figured I'd make us all some popcorn before it played.

Midway through the popping, I heard Dr. Hook instead of Neil Young, and I knew for an irrefutable fact that they conspired to change the record when I left the room because they didn't want to confront me.

Well I'll goddamned show you. I'm out here doing you a fucking favor, and you choose now to fuck with me. You know the rest.

Of course, the story in the other room was just as wrong. Oh, he left to make popcorn, so I guess he doesn't care to hear Mister Young after all. Switch it.

And of course, they're completely wrong, and I'm completely right because that's how the vain judge themselves, isn't it now? Turns out, we're all wrong. I've never met a man who's cornered the market on truth, and I don't suspect I ever will. Hell, I'd never see him coming anyway. Only saints and disciples see that sort of thing, and I'm neither.

I'm also happy to report that our place doesn't need any fixing. It just seemed that way at the time. But you sure learn that what things seem to be and what things really are aren't just different sides of the same coin. They're different currency.

I guess what I'm getting to is this:

Over the years, I've gotten better and better at re-pair-by-apology. I think I used to try to rip things apart—I'm talking about relationships here—and rebuild them better than I imagined they were. The older I get, the more I see that for what it is: vanity. And the vain have a devil of a time saying I'm sorry. Here's my modest advice: watch out for that. Especially in yourself. It can save you a whole lot of trouble.

BRIAN SORRELL MOVED FROM CALIFORNIA TO NEW ZEALAND IN 2012 and enjoys a beachy life as a stay-at-home dad. He is a regular contributor to MerelyMothers.com, KiwiFamilies.co.nz, and he created DaddingFullTime.com. His writings have also appeared in literary journals, academic journals, and a variety of online venues.

I Can't Believe You Ate My Sandwich

By Kathryn Leehane

THE FIRST BIG FIGHT MY HUSBAND AND I GOT INTO WAS over a sandwich. This argument happened almost twenty years ago, and I still haven't quite forgiven him.

You see, I have food issues. In my family, mealtime was a war zone, and as the youngest of six kids, I was generally the loser. We kids fought for every piece of food and ate as quickly as possible in order not to go hungry. On the very rare occasions that my father bought fast food, we would fight over every French fry on our plates. He only bought three boxes of fries for six kids, so we actually had to count individual French fries to ensure even distribution.

My husband knew about my history. I had relayed the battle stories. I had shown him the scars. He had seen the damage early in our dating years when we went out to lunch with some friends. When I got up to get more napkins, one of our friends reached over to take one of my French fries. My soon-to-be husband laughed hysterically as I nearly ripped my friend's head off with a verbal assault of vitriol and damnation. Over a French fry.

I'm also picky. The seedy and watery residue from one tomato can ruin an entire burger. I'd rather cover my body in mayonnaise than eat one bite of it. I still have flashbacks from the time my parents threatened me with corporal punishment if I did not eat a taco salad drowning in French dressing. (I opted for the swat on the backside over choking down that sickly-sweet liquid horror.)

So I made my demands known early on. I came with clear handling instructions. My husband went into this relationship completely aware—or perhaps in denial. Maybe he just needed more practice, because he clearly wasn't ready for the Great Sandwich Tragedy.

It happened a few months before we got married. We had traveled to Portland, Oregon so that I could interview for a major manufacturing company. I was incredibly nervous about the interview. Up until this point, I had been working at a university teaching computer workshops, which seemed like the Little Leagues compared to the high-tech industry.

I labored over my wardrobe choice. I debated how I should wear my hair, how much makeup I should apply, which pens made me look the most intellectual. I spent hours packing and preparing for that trip. I was furiously reading up on the company history and all of the products they manufactured. I needed to sound like an expert.

I was a nervous wreck.

We flew in on a weekday morning. I hadn't slept much the prior night, so I was exhausted. At the time, Portland International Airport was called "Little Beirut" because the construction had turned it into a war zone. We got lost on the way to the rental car place.

I was now nervous, exhausted, and a bit irritated.

Once we secured our car, we proceeded to drive to our hotel. The airport and our hotel were on completely opposite sides of the city—a good forty-five minutes and four freeways away.

Him: "You want to stop for anything to eat?"

Me: "No, let's just get to the hotel, so I can do more interview prep."

Naturally, we went the wrong way on one of the freeways and ended up going the opposite direction of our hotel. We calmly turned around and worked together with our MapQuest printouts.

"We are a *team*," I told myself through clenched teeth. We finally navigated our way through the labyrinth of confusing bridges and freeways and after a couple of hours had managed to find our hotel.

At that point, I was getting super hungry. Maybe a little hangry[1].

---

1   *hangry (adj.): irritable as a result of feeling hungry*

As we pulled into the hotel, we noticed a sandwich shop nearby. We decided to grab some sandwiches and drinks to bring with us to our hotel room. Although I was nervous, exhausted, irritable, *and* famished, I carefully placed my order: a turkey sandwich with extra pickles, peppers, and mustard. NO mayonnaise.

We checked in and went immediately to our room. I had to use the facilities, and my husband got lunch ready (and by "got lunch ready," I mean unwrapped the sandwiches and laid them out on the hotel coffee table). When I came out of the bathroom, he was sitting in front of the television eating a sandwich. I grabbed the other sandwich and sat down beside him. I was *ravenous*.

Him: "Sorry I started without you. I was starving."

Me: "No problem. I am too."

And with that, I started eating. I took one bite and immediately gagged. I spit out the sandwich piece and the words, "What the fuck? This isn't my sandwich!"

Him: "What? Of course that's your sandwich. I'm eating mine."

Me: "What's in your sandwich?"

Him: "Turkey, pickles—"

Me (interrupting): "Is there any MAYO on your sandwich?"

Him: "I don't know. Yes?"

Me: "YOU DON'T KNOW? Open it up."

I performed a sandwich autopsy right then and there on the coffee table.

Me: "There's no mayo in this sandwich! And THIS one [holding 'my' sandwich like it was a soiled diaper] has mayo ALL OVER IT!"

Him: "Oh my god, I'm sorry."

Me: "Sorry? SORRY? You ate my fucking sandwich."

He held out the remaining third of the sandwich he was eating, "Here. Eat this."

So then I was nervous, exhausted, irritated, hangry, AND insulted.

Me: "THAT IS NOT ENOUGH SANDWICH FOR ME!"

Him: "Well then eat mine."

Me: "I CAN'T EAT ANYTHING WITH MAYO OR TOMA-TOES. HOW DID YOU NOT NOTICE YOU WERE EATING MY SANDWICH?"

Him: "I was hungry. I thought I grabbed mine."

At that point, I became irrational.

Me: "HOW COULD YOU NOT NOTICE? HOW COULD YOU EAT MY FUCKING SANDWICH?"

Him: "I'll go get you another one."

Me: "No. I'll just scrape off all of this crap from YOUR sandwich and try to eat it."

Him: "You're not going to be a sandwich martyr. Let me go get you another sandwich."

Me: "I DON'T WANT A NEW SANDWICH. I WANT MY OLD SANDWICH."

Him: "Oh my god. Take the remaining sandwich, and I'll go get you another one."

I ate the remaining portion (and the next sandwich) and eventually calmed down enough to nail that job interview and get the job. We lived very happily in Portland for almost thirteen years.

But I never trusted my husband with any sandwiches again. In fact, for many years after, I conducted mandatory Sandwich Inspections before anyone was allowed to take a bite. That involved laying out sandwiches side by side and meticulously comparing ingredients. Only after I had conducted and approved the Sandwich Identification Process (SIP) would I reassemble the sandwiches and redistribute them. *It was my job.*

Several years after the Great Sandwich Tragedy of 1997, we had kids. Because of those kids, I'm not nearly as picky or possessive of food anymore. I've mostly forgiven my husband, but I've not forgotten. No, I'll never forget.

Whenever there is an injustice or a slight of any kind (not just food-related), I just mumble, "I can't believe you ate my sandwich."

KATHRYN LEEHANE IS A MOM AND A WRITER LIVING IN THE SAN Francisco Bay Area with her husband and two children. After too many years in high tech, she finally decided to follow her true passion. She is working on her first book, and she writes the humor blog, Foxy Wine Pocket, where she shares twisted stories about her life as a mother, wife, friend, and wine-drinker in suburbia. Irreverent, inappropriate, and just plain silly, Kathryn strives to make you spit out your drink (wine, right?). Her essays have also been featured on BLUNTmoms, Scary Mommy, The Huffington Post, and in various anthologies. In her down time, she inhales books, bacon, and Pinot Noir, and her interests include over-sharing, Jason Bateman, and crashing high school reunions.

The Unwilling Passenger

By April Grant

HAVE YOU EVER HAD A FIGHT WITH YOUR SPOUSE THAT you were ultimately glad you lost? Yeah, me neither. Thankfully, that's not the tale I'm here to tell you today.

This story starts out with two parents, who get along relatively well, and a son who wants to visit his aunt. This might seem odd, but his aunt is only two months younger. Yes, that's us. However, this story isn't about the adventures of two adorable kids.

This story is about a family who is ultra-cool, loving, heartwarming, and, well, not my family. I try not to talk about my family too much. In the past, they've been slightly disappointing, to say the least. Here's just one example and what this story is really all about:

My son recently wanted to travel to visit my mother. For some, this might not be a problem. Grandmothers love their grandkids! The problem is that my mother is more likely to have my son work in her business than she is spending time spoiling him. The first time they spent grandmother-grandson time together, she came to visit after not seeing him for over three years *and* incessantly commenting that she hadn't spent time with her grandson. After they spent a full day together (about 8:00 a.m. to 4:00 p.m.), I asked him what they did for fun.

Him: "I read."

Me: "You mean, Grandma read to you?"

Him: "No, I read my book."

Me: "What did Grandma do?"

Him: "She played on the computer."

Me: "Hmmm." (It was my way of silently saying this will *never* happen again.)

At the end of the day, she mentioned that they'd had a great time together. *Really? Which part was great? Was it him reading to himself or you working on your computer?* I thought to myself.

I tried to be open-minded. So a couple years later, when she came to visit, she asked to spend time with him again. This time would not be alone grandmother-grandson time; my sister would be there too. They're the same age, so if she can find something fun to do with my sister, she can find something for my son. In our area, things are pretty cheap, so doubling the price might be twenty dollars, instead of the ten dollars she might have been expecting.

This time, I actually had to work, and my son had the day off from school. I dropped him off at the house she was staying at on my way into work.

When I returned later that day, I noticed that my mother's friend was there. Thankfully, this was a girlfriend and not a guy friend, so none of those questions ran through my mind. I casually asked, "How long has Stephanie been here?"

My mother responded without hesitation, "Oh, she came over before lunch. We've spent the day catching up!"

So there I was, after my son having a "reading" grandma-grandson day the last time and now, a few years later, my mother begging for my son to spend time with her again, wondering *What for?* On her second opportunity to be a grandmother, she spent it talking to her friend, while my sister and son played in the bedroom.

Three years later, I wanted to try it again. I wanted to see if she had changed.

Because of the history, I asked my husband, "Should we do this?"

His response, surprisingly, was, "Why not?" My husband couldn't come up with an immediate objection. He's so much more rational than I am and kaput, nothing, complete ready agreement.

Oh my goodness, I'm actually going to send my son to spend a week with my mother.

About a month before my son was to visit his grandmother, I made plans to drive him there to save money. My husband's family was worried about me making the drive alone, so they asked around to see who would be willing to make the trip with me. It turned out, everyone had things to do. So as not to upset his parents, my husband volunteered to go with me on the four-hundred-mile drive.

As we were getting ourselves, our son, and one daughter packed and ready to go, my husband pulled me aside and said, "I'm never doing this again."

Really? WTH? I was so taken aback that I didn't say anything at the time. I'm not even sure where he was coming from or what was going through his head.

He spoke softly as he reiterated, "I'll drive with you this time, but I won't do it again."

"I didn't ask you to do it this time. I could've done it alone. I don't need your pity company, I mean accompaniment." Yep, when I'm upset, I use ten-dollar words. It really makes our arguments seamless.

On our way out the door, my husband began listing the reasons that I should *not* be making this trip: not trusting my mother, not considering her an attentive mother, and hoping that she doesn't leave my son to his own devices during the visit. These were all valid points. Valid points that would have made more sense to bring up weeks before leaving, instead of as we put our last bag in the car.

What exactly did he want me to do with this information on such late notice? Of course, I brought up all of the counter points: she's older now, she's more mature, and well, she's wiser now, so she can't make the same mistakes again, *could she?* Plus, the kids were in the car, my mother was expecting us, my other daughter was with my in-laws, and I had already driven ten miles in the rental car. I was pretty sure they didn't give you a full refund after driving the car off the lot. Therefore, I was fully committed to making this trip.

I presented that seemingly wonderfully crafted argument. My husband simply responded that he'd go on this trip, no problem—it was the next one he wasn't going on. Since this was a done deal, I shut my mouth and embarked on a wonderful trip up the east coast.

My son ended up having a great time. My mother was apparently very involved and attentive. They even caught a shark—a long story for another day. Maybe next time, my husband will actually want to come along. And be a willing passenger.

APRIL GRANT IS A WIFE AND MOTHER OF FOUR (ONE BOY ON EARTH, one in heaven, and two girls). As a lawyer turned stay-at-home mother, she writes about her life and researches ways to make it easier for herself and others. Her children bring her the ultimate joy, even when the girls don't sleep through the night! Follow her journey at 100lb Countdown.

By Bev Feldman

Never Assume Anything

By Bev Feldman

I F YOU'RE EVER LOOKING FOR A GOOD WAY TO REALLY TEST the limits of a brand-new marriage, then I suggest that you and your new spouse quit your jobs and spend nearly half a year together, constantly at one another's side, often relying on one another for comfort and entertainment.

I know what you're thinking. *Are you crazy? Who would want to do that?*

Well that's how my husband, Sam, and I spent a good chunk of our first year as a married couple. In December of 2011, after being married just over three months, Sam and I said goodbye to our jobs, our apartment, family, friends, and our cat and embarked on an almost six-month journey around South America.

The trip, of course, was absolutely incredible, and we are so grateful to have been able to do it. But let me tell you, in the day-to-day, it really was not as glamorous as it may sound. Sure, we got to eat new and interesting foods (who knew llama tasted like a cross between beef and pork?), go on some pretty epic adventures, meet cool people from around the world, and learn first-hand about different cultures. But nothing will induce more marriage-related breakdowns than practically being joined at the hip with your new spouse for any period of time longer than a typical honeymoon.

Given how much time we spent together and that we constantly had to communicate in Spanish (of which neither one of us were native speakers), disasters were inevitable. From grumpiness over cramped and uncomfortable quarters to freak-outs over death-defying drives, we had our moments that would make even the most pissed-off toddler proud.

Perhaps, though, the one that most sticks out in my mind involves an international flight, visiting in-laws, and an unlicensed cab driver.

First, there is one thing to know about traveling around South America (and something which I found myself constantly reminding Sam): never assume anything.

Never assume the bus company will have an electronic copy of your ticket; never assume that your train will leave anywhere near the scheduled time (or that there will be anyone around to tell you when it will even arrive); never assume you will stop for a bathroom break on a seven-hour bus ride through hellishly bumpy and unpaved roads; never assume that a touristy but remote area will have an

ATM when you don't have enough cash with you; and most importantly, never assume that your international flight will leave from the international airport. If you all you do is follow this one basic rule, you will save you and your partner from a great deal of unnecessary stress. (But mostly you, because you are getting tired of repeating yourself.)

After several months of frustrating situations caused by making false assumptions, you would think by our third month into the trip we would have learned this very important lesson. But unfortunately, you would be mistaken.

Let me set the scene:

After a particularly interesting stint volunteering on a farm just outside Buenos Aires, where for two weeks we shared a tiny cabin with four roommates and an endless army of ants, we were thrilled to return to civilization (a.k.a. the city) and enjoy a beautiful one-bedroom apartment with hot showers and some privacy. For four whole days, I might add! After that, we were joined by my sister, who spent a week with us, until an hour before Sam's parents who then joined us to stay for two weeks.

Now I have to tell you, I have the most wonderful in-laws. They are the sweetest, most loving people, and I truly enjoy spending time with them. But staying with anyone's parents for two straight weeks (while technically on your honeymoon), when your bedroom is the living room, gets a little old after a while. And after nearly five weeks in the same tiny apartment, I was getting antsy and ready for a change of scenery.

Thankfully, as I was reaching the end of my rope and really starting to crave some privacy, we decided to embark on the next leg of the journey and make our way to Santiago, Chile.

The night before our flight, in self-conscious Spanish, I reserved a van to take us all to the international airport on the outskirts of the city, about a forty-five-minute ride without traffic for our early-morning flight. As Sam had booked the flight, he double-checked the flight details, and we figured out what time we would need to leave to ensure ample time to check in and go through security.

I'll admit, I'm a pretty neurotic travel companion, especially if there are flights involved. I want to be at the airport at least two hours in advance of an international flight departing, and if we're running more than five minutes behind schedule, seething starts to ensue with the occasional colorful word (directed, of course, at Sam), and, if you're really lucky, some foot stamping.

Amazingly, our van arrived at exactly the time I had requested, around 6:00 a.m. the next morning. Since it was still early, we made it to the airport in plenty of time, and I was feeling the epitome of the calm, seasoned traveler.

However, despite being at the check-in desk nearly two hours before our scheduled boarding time, we were told it was too late to check into our flight.

At this point, I could feel my anxiety level starting to rise. We double-checked the time of our flight, and in Sam's even more broken Spanish, he tried to figure out why our flight would leave earlier than the scheduled time. After much confusion, we finally figured out the problem: we were at the wrong airport.

In checking the details of our flight, Sam had neglected to double-check the airport we were leaving from, and had assumed our international flight to Chile would leave from the international airport, when it was actually leaving from the airport that is primarily for domestic flights. (See what happens when you make assumptions?)

With the clock ticking away, we had about an hour and a half to drive *back* into the city to get to the other airport, and both my anxiety and anger were reaching dangerously high levels. Conveniently, there was a man standing nearby who asked if we needed a cab. With our massive luggage in tow, Sam, his mom and dad, and I hurriedly followed the man to his cab, which was really just a regular car parked in the lot. As we were losing precious minutes, we didn't stop to question whether this was a legitimate cab or not.

We pulled out onto the highway, only to be met immediately with a massive amount of traffic. Unlike us, the rest of Argentina had work to get to. At this point, my pissed-off-o-meter (totally a thing) was in code red.

Now normally, when Sam's parents are around, I am able to tone down my frustration with Sam (or at least hide it). Not at that moment. For the entire ride, as our crazy (and most certainly illegitimate) cab driver wove in between cars, coming dangerously close to swiping at least a few of them, I sat sandwiched between Sam's parents in the backseat, absolutely seething at Sam. At one point, Sam's dad tried to make me feel better. He gently placed his hand on my arm and told me it would be okay.

Through gritted teeth, I told him in the calmest tone I could muster, *"Please … don't … touch … me … right … now."*

The whole ride, all I could think about was how pissed I was and that we were going to miss our flight. (We'll just ignore the fact that there were still plenty of other flights we could catch to Santiago. That wasn't the point.) When I'm that pissed, there is no calming me down, no matter how irrational my anger might be.

Finally, with definitely less than an hour to go until our flight's scheduled departure time, the cab driver dropped us off at the correct airport. Sam told his parents and me to start checking in while he paid the cab driver (who, by the way, charged us nearly double what it had cost our first ride—and which added more fire to my freak-out when I found out). We dashed through the airport—of course, the driver had let us off on the other end of the airport from where our airline was located—while I silently cursed at Sam and this whole trip.

By some amazing grace of good fortune, when we reached the ticket counter, panting and sweating, we found out that our flight had been delayed, and we were able to still check in for it. We made it through security, tensions and everyone's heartbeats high, with about five minutes to spare until they started boarding our plane.

Even though it all worked out, I was too worked up and refused to talk to Sam for the entire flight. It took until we landed in Santiago for my tantrum to end and for me to feel calm enough to talk to Sam (and his parents, who were just innocent bystanders) again.

Although I was pissed as hell at the time and was definitely in no mood to find anything funny, in retrospect I find the whole ordeal hilarious. I realized what a crazed person I turn into if I feel I'm running late for a flight (which, shockingly, Sam still seems to have yet to learn). Plus, it's just part of the adventure of traveling around as newlyweds in foreign countries.

More than anything, despite all the moments of frustration and having times when were just plain sick of each other's company, we realized that if we could spend *that much* time with each other that soon into our marriage, then we would be okay in the long run. As long as Sam checks our flight information properly.

AFTER RETURNING FROM HER UNCONVENTIONAL HONEYMOON backpacking around South America, Bev Feldman was inspired to put her career in education on hold and focus on her jewelry business and blogging. She lives in the Boston area with Sam and their daughter. You can check out Bev's jewelry and writing on her website, Linkouture.

The Aluminum Can Incident

By Jodi Crafts-Flaherty

I'VE BEEN WITH MY HUSBAND, CHUCK, FOR MORE THAN twelve years. Although we had polar opposite childhoods, we are unbelievably similar and well-matched—perfectly paired in political and religious beliefs, even ideally matched zodiac signs. We are both middle children and tend to steer toward finding common ground rather than debating. Both of us are very mild-mannered in personality (which of course is why our children came out so stubborn; *someone* has to make decisions). When Chuck and I actually have a disagreement, two things usually happen: we might quietly discuss and resolve the issue, or if really intense, we may walk away and table it for later.

We do have some minor challenges: competitive board games. Did you know there is a phone number to solve disputes in *Trivial Pursuit*? There is, and we tried to use it.

For the record, I was right. Although I don't know if we technically got an official answer on it—just trust me, I was right.

Housekeeping priorities is another difference—but we wouldn't discover that one right away. Some might consider our relationship dull, rarely having a healthy debate. We do, we just respect the other's opinions and are open to listening. We also survived a period of bigger marital issues, making us stronger in our commitment. Even through these worst of times, we still found compromise. It is just in our nature, as a couple.

When Chuck and I moved into our first house, it was old and tiny. I was on an instant mission to be the best round-the-clock hostess and wife you could possibly envision. We took on certain unspoken roles. Chuck would never clean a toilet, and I admittedly had difficulty with most yard work. I cooked; he barbequed. We shared the laundry and loading the dishwasher. I would never describe Chuck as sloppy; he just prioritizes cleaning differently. With two jobs and limited time to relax, cleaning is just not high on his list. First, it was leaving clothes just outside the hamper or shoes strewn across the middle of the floor. Then I would discover damp towels on my side of the bed. Finally, dishes and empty soda cans were left casually by the sink. Still, I proudly cleaned and kept a silent tally.

When we gathered with his family, my two sisters-in-law and I would rib our husbands about the laziness we encountered in front of their mom. We laughed and one-upped each other with our stories.

Sister-in-law #1: "No matter where I move the laundry basket, my husband seems to miss it."

Sister-in-law #2: "Well, my husband just leaves piles of clothes in the closet."

Me: "Chuck has clothes that he swears are clean sharing space with the pile of dirty clothes on the floor. Apparently, I should be able to recognize the difference."

We laugh, drink some wine, and continue on like this, always inviting our mother-in-law to share her stories too—a benefit gained with three daughters-in-law. She promises she taught her three boys to clean up after themselves and sometimes shares a story or two of her own humorous housekeeping tribulations from her marriage. I always found it rather therapeutic to have these shared moments. Or so I thought.

I am embarrassed to tell you about the day I nearly cracked-up. It was over something so silly, yet it all felt monumental at the time. I had reached my boiling point. I wish I could say it was over something truly epic, something meaningful, but no, it was just a symbolic aluminum can. Well, in actuality, *many* of them.

One hot summer day, we hosted a gathering, and I spent the next morning cleaning the house and rinsing aluminum cans. A lot of them. After the house was restored to a fairly pristine condition, I went on about my day. I'm really not sure of all of the details, as the memory includes moments of blur. However, I do remember finding the kitchen sink with several additional dirty cans in and around it. As I stared at these cans, I began to grow beyond angry. They were just left for me to clean. Sitting there demanding that I rinse them.

I grew up in an old house that regularly suffered the seasonal ambush of ants. I was stuck with images of these ants and my mother tirelessly working to rid the house of them. I lost a beloved Easter basket filled with candy to an army of those damn tyrants. I'm not afraid of ants. I am just highly irritated by bugs, in general. I should let you know, that was twenty-five-plus years ago, and ants have not been problematic for me in *any* recent years.

Nonetheless, I began to silently embody someone who could only be described as Crazy Eyes from *Orange is the New Black* crossed with a slightly less enraged version of *Mommy Dearest*. I just waited for Chuck to come into the kitchen from a nearby room, where I had seen him trying to relax. When he did approach, I immediately burst in tears, possibly began drooling, and rambled on and on about ants.

Chuck rightfully didn't expect any of this. Although I am at times emotional, this was a whole different level. I angrily rinsed cans, threw some of them in the trash, and a lucky few made it into the recycling bin. All of this was in between my tears and totally irrational fits of incoherent words about bugs.

"We are going to get ants, all over the house!"

"I am not a maid!"

"I do not have child!" (We didn't at this time.)

"Do you know how gross this is?"

"I don't want ants in my food!"

"Did you seriously leave these here for me?"

Yada, yada yada—you get the picture. Just add in your visions of sweat, lots of tears, and a tiny blonde having body tremors.

Chuck suggested we "just throw the cans away—perhaps recycling was just not worth this." Whoa, his suggestion did not help. He was missing my point and completely baffled (as he should have been) by this bizarre reaction. I imagine I sounded like the parent voice from *Charlie Brown* to him. My tantrum, as it could only be described, included curse words about aluminum and possibly me crushing a few cans. I can remember the heat and flow of the tears. I recall Chuck standing there helpless and quiet, patiently waiting for my tirade to end and not wanting to provoke it further or, heaven help him, laugh. When my emotional outburst finally subsided, he hugged me and apologized (probably very confused as why he had to apologize).

In our marriage, this has simply become known as "the aluminum can incident." In retrospect, it was very embarrassing and a little funny. I have never let myself get so passive that I exploded again. I know it was about more than ants and empty cans. It was about stopping that silly, silent tally and communicating better with one another. Forgiving and moving past the little things that in the big picture of marriage actually amount to nothing. I appreciate that he is a far better partner in so many other truly important ways (though that damp towel thing *still* irks me). I also know that sometimes I need take time to *relax* with him. The cleaning will wait, and with two young children, it is never truly complete anyway. Now I gladly nag (only if needed), and he is very aware that it's better if I do. On a pleasant note, ants have not ever been a huge issue in our home. We also very rarely drink soda out of cans. Let's just say, it's probably better for our marriage that way.

FORMERLY OF MASSACHUSETTS, JODI CRAFTS-FLAHERTY MET HER husband in Iowa and currently spends her days chasing two wild, little boys. She is educated in travel, marketing, real estate, and cosmetology. A coffee connoisseur with a developing interest in "going green," Jodi is living her dream and being raised by her family. She blogs at The Noise of Boys, where she details daily lessons in motherhood and parenting and all the laughter that it brings.

Escape of the Chocolate Placenta

By Scott Rigdon

WHEN MY WIFE WAS PREGNANT WITH OUR FIRST child, we spent countless hours planning the birth. I was fortunate enough to deliver our son myself, in a birthing tub in the comfort of our own living room.

As wonderful as that sounds, and was, it did not at all go as planned. After twenty-six hours of labor, my wife was completely exhausted and couldn't push anymore. It was time to give up on the home birth and get an ambulance on the way. I'm glad that we had a midwife there to break that news to her; my wife had her heart set on having a natural childbirth in our home.

As that discussion unfolded in front of me, I realized that my little man was in fact still attempting to enter our world. You know how the head is supposed to crown first? Well, not my little man! He reached out his right hand to wave hello! When I reached down to touch his tiny hand, he grabbed my pinky and held on for dear life. I was having the most amazing experience of my existence. After more than three long years of attempting to create a baby, here he was, and he was holding my hand for the first time. At that moment, the reality of fatherhood hit me like a brick. Time slowed to a crawl, and I savored the moment.

I said, "He's holding my hand, and he has a killer grip!" The midwife immediately came to my aid, and started working with his arm.

My wife asked confused, "He's really holding your hand? How? Is he out?"

"Just his arm," replied the midwife.

I thought this was the moment at which my wife would also share in my dreamy joy, as we witnessed the miracle of our son's first interaction with us outside of the womb. Unfortunately, I had mistaken the look on her face for one of awe and amazement, when in fact it was a look of disbelief at my stupidity.

"If he's holding your hand that tight, then PULL HIM OUT, you fucking idiot!"

Now, I'd been to all the boot camps for childbirth and new parents. I wasn't surprised, offended, or hurt at all by the swearing. I'd been warned to expect just about anything during childbirth. However, the yelling did snap all of us out of our starry-eyed moment, and as I prepared to give my little man a hefty tug to help him gain access to our living room, the midwife jumped in with a big, NO-NO-NO wave and took over the hand-holding. She performed some sort of magic trick that unraveled his arm from around his neck while simultaneously bringing him all the way out to meet us.

I had the privilege of handing him to my wife at that point, and he milked that show like a pro! He cooed and blew bubbles and nuzzled his mom. The rest of the birth went as it was supposed to, and I found myself shortly thereafter holding his placenta.

It was beautiful. It wasn't like the ones I'd seen in the pictures, and even the midwife agreed that it was unique. I asked the midwife what they typically do with the after-birth, and she said they typically send it as bio-waste to wherever they send the liner from the birthing tub. She also explained that some people keep the placenta and plant a tree over it for the sake of doing something meaningful. That sounded like a great idea, and while the midwife cleaned up the tub and my wife slept, I found an empty ice cream bucket in which to store my son's placenta. I tucked it away in the bottom of our deep freezer. I mentioned it to my wife the next day, and she agreed that we should plant a tree over it. Little did I know, the placenta had other plans and was already devising an escape route.

Nearly a year later, a somewhat unexpected job opportunity left us scrambling to move in only a few days' time. I went down to the new job before the movers came, while my wife coordinated the move itself. We spoke every night on the phone, and I'll never forget the final call we shared when she and our boy had vacated the old place and were headed my way to meet me at the new house. She was already *en route* when she called, and the conversation went something like this:

"So the place is empty? That's kinda sad," I said.

My wife replied, "Yeah. It is. I just gave away all of the food in the fridge to the neighbors. I didn't want to deal with packing it in a cooler and then unpacking it. A bunch of them came over to help while the movers were here, so I just told them to take whatever looked good to them from the fridge and the freezer."

I lamented, "Our son was born in that house. It's hard to leave." And then it hit me. "Hey, wait ... what did you do with his placenta?"

Silence followed for some time. Finally she responded, "Oh yeah. We kept his placenta. Where was it?"

"In the bottom of the freezer. The deep freezer, not the refrigerator freezer. In an old chocolate ice cream bucket," I replied.

Another long period of silence followed. She was obviously scrambling to remember who took what from where. "I have no idea. The fridge and deep freeze were empty when the movers loaded them. One of the neighbors probably thought it was ice cream and took it home with them!"

Now, I'll spare you the details of the argument that followed. It was my fault that I left my son's placenta in an ice cream bucket in our freezer for a year. It was her fault that she forgot it was in there and gave it away. It was my fault because I wasn't there to help with the move. It was her fault because she should have remembered. It was both our faults, but at the time, we were so upset about losing the placenta that we didn't see it that way.

The next day, she called all of the neighbors who had been there helping. No one could locate the placenta. I have to assume that possibly one of them took it and tossed it out thinking it was old ice cream, or one of them opened the bucket and was so traumatized about what they found in there that they didn't want to admit they had it. In any case, the placenta was lost that day, and no tree was ever planted over it.

In the end, it was all my fault. Because I was the husband. Sometimes a husband or wife has to take one for the team. I took the heat for that one, yet I never really lived it down. Regardless of who was at fault, we argued about it on and off for some time after. Eventually, we were both just deeply saddened that we never knew the fate of the placenta. I like to think it's on a warm beach somewhere tropical, sipping fruity drinks, sharing the details of its masterminded escape with the locals.

A tree planted over our placenta would have been a great story to tell. But one that escaped our home disguised as leftover chocolate ice cream? That's a story that will be told by our great-great-grandchildren.

By Scott Rigdon

SCOTT RIGDON IS STILL FIGURING OUT WHO HE IS, BUT HE HAS always enjoyed writing. Before he had kids, he wrote articles about car and four-by-four outings and attended many car-club events. Once that first positive pregnancy test came along, the topic of his writing shifted markedly toward babies! As the kids muddled through their toddler years, he also became a single parent, and for lots of reasons, the focus of his writing became centered on family outings. Now that they're approaching their teens, the stories have more depth, the funny things have become often hilarious, and the sharp retorts are sometimes both profound and surprising. Scott is finding that he has no end of things to write about on his blog, Three Five Zero. He's also found that he learns just as much from his kids as he teaches them. Those are the stories he loves to write the most.

Corn Hole and Fried Dough

By Lydia Richmond

I HAVE THE ABILITY TO ARGUE WITH MY HUSBAND WITHOUT words. Really, it's like a magical power that I have.

The first time my husband and I ever fought, it was because he tried to help me clean. But it wasn't the sort of helping that included picking up the trash or wiping the counters. He had decided that he would help me organize my office closet—his way.

Now, let me explain my office closet. It's not in any way organized to the outsider's eye, but in my mind, it makes perfect sense. This box is filled with tons of markers meant specifically for scrapbooking. That box is filled with tons of markers, pencils, and other types of writing utensils solely for our children to use. While it may appear that I just have multiple boxes of markers, they are organized and match my brain. I remember where they are, and I can find them pretty quickly when needed.

To Aaron, it's not the same. He just saw boxes upon boxes of junk and thought to himself, "Well, it's all crafty junk. It can just live together." With that, he dumped all of my little boxes of organized chaos into one large plastic box of disorganized madness.

Take a moment and really think about this with me. He had dropped all of my seemingly disorganized, cluttered life into one big box. No longer would I easily find my scrapbooking paper or my fancy scissors or the guitar strings I'd been meaning to put on my barely-used guitar.

He came into the living room and showed me what he'd done. My eyes widened, and I yelled with exasperation, "Why did you do that? Don't ever touch my office closet!" I didn't think it was too much to ask, and I certainly didn't think that I was saying anything offensive.

His response was to the point and was something like, "Well, don't ask me to ever do anything for you again."

I sat there, stunned.

We'd never argued about anything more than which ice cream flavor we should purchase. I slid back down on the couch cushions and melted into a puddle of silent tears. In perfect Aaron form, he had no clue. He just kept on moving things around in the office.

I stewed in my hurt and anger. All of the complaints I could think of about him welled up inside of me.

He never asks me before he does something.

He doesn't think my things are important.

He wants to get rid of all of my things.

He doesn't really love me.

A few moments later, he finally realized that I was upset. He came around the front of the couch to see me wiping away tears and sniffling without noise. He lowered his brow and was clearly confused.

In a very surprised voice he asked, "Are you crying?"

"You borderline yelled at me!" I said, and he just chuckled. Chuckled! And then I chuckled, too, at such a ridiculous thing to say to him.

This is what happens when you allow an online dating service to match you. If they do a really good job, you're paired with someone who truly complements you. Aaron is my perfect complement. I have always said that he is the missing puzzle piece to my crazy self.

Where I am red-blooded and easily angered, he's completely chilled and relaxed. Did the entire office closet ordeal bother him? Not one bit. In fact, after he "borderline yelled" at me, he forgot about the entire exchange until he realized I was upset.

This is pretty much how all of our fights go down. We've been married for five years and have known each other for a little over six. In that time, we've had maybe three real arguments. Most of them go about the same way: he does something, I get upset that it wasn't what I wanted, I get huffy, and he is clueless. I huff and puff about it for about a week, and then, in a moment of hurried explanation, I tell him that I've been mad at him for the past week. He's usually surprised.

Our biggest fight to date happened after he was gone for a day to watch NASCAR. This is a time when he and his buddies meet up to tailgate before going to watch grown men in cars driving around in circles. I have been with him twice, and I tried very hard to like it. The tailgating? That was fun. I like food. The race part? Not so much. I know that if I go in the future, I just need to take a book. Ho-hum.

So this past year, I sent him on his own and told him not to worry about little old me sitting at home with our baby, toddler, and tween. I'd be fine. No worries here.

Until I developed some weird stomach-cramping disease and thought I'd never walk again. To make matters worse, my mother (who is usually my backup) was unavailable.

As he left for the race, he kissed me on my forehead, told me he hoped I felt better, and was gone. I walked around helping my babies play while doubled over in pain. Nothing sounded good. Nothing tasted good. I didn't want to do anything but sleep.

Somehow, I finally made it through naptimes (when yes, I did, uncharacteristically, take a nap), dinner, baths, and bedtimes. When they went to bed, I crawled into my own bed and stayed there. And I stewed in my anger at Aaron, who had done exactly what I told him to do—he went to watch the race and have fun with his friends.

He got home late that night as expected, but when he joined me in bed, I gave him the cold shoulder. Once again, every complaint I could think of began running through my head:

How dare he go to the race?

He doesn't love me enough to give up those expensive seats.

He likes his friends more than he likes me.

He hates me.

It took me forever to fall asleep that night. He had no trouble, as he was exhausted from a full day of corn hole and fried dough. I tossed and turned and silently cursed him.

For another few days, I was angry with him. I didn't speak as warmly to him as I normally do. I hugged him but rather begrudgingly. When he tried to talk to me, I smiled a half smile and listened politely. I was angry at him for not realizing how sick I was the day of the race and fixing it right then and there.

Forget that I had told him to go to the race anyway.

Forget that I survived, and nothing bad had happened.

Forget that I was being a child and pouting.

It finally bothered me so much that I felt like I needed to talk to him. He needed to hear me say that my feelings had been hurt and that I had been angry at him.

While we lay in bed talking, I said, "I need you to know that I've been mad at you all week."

He sort of did a double-take and said, "What? Why?"

See? He had absolutely no clue that I had been upset. The entire time, I'd been fighting with myself.

We laughed as I told him why I had been angry, and he explained that he couldn't very well fix anything if I didn't tell him how I'd felt. The whole week of anger washed right out of my system, and I felt tons better.

Fights in this house are usually only heard between the children. Obviously, Aaron and I fight in a much different way. He's silent. I'm pouty.

This is how I know that he's perfect for me. In past relationships, the drama and screaming and crying took over the happiness. I know that it's important for couples to air their frustrations so they don't fester and explode later. We're still doing that. We just don't have the knock-down, drag-out fights and scenes that others experience.

Will he go to the race again this year? Oh yes. He will. Everyone needs to do their thing, and he really does enjoy hanging out with his friends.

Will he organize something of mine only to get an earfull from me about not touching my stuff? Oh yes. This is an absolute certainty. After all, you should see my desk. It's riddled with the most obnoxious piles of clutter. Our kitchen counters are similar. You'd think I had no element of organization, but it's there. Really, it is.

I've learned how to handle it when he borderline yells at me. At least, I think I have. I just have the fight in my head and let us say all the dramatic, loud things to each other there and then let him know how it turns out. That works for us.

LYDIA RICHMOND IS A STAY-AT-HOME, WORK-AT-HOME MOM OF three (Miss Sassy Pants, The Animal, and Flash) and wife to Aaron, a high school math teacher. After teaching high school English face-to-face for eleven years, Lydia chose to stay home and teach online to both high schoolers and community college students. In 2013, she published her first children's book, *A Day to Remember*. When she's not chasing a baby, tutoring a student, or doing the laundry, Lydia enjoys sitting still on the couch with her man watching whatever they have on DVR. Hang out with Lydia on her blog, Cluttered Genius.

What About Them is Not Identical?

By Allie Burdick

"UM, WHAT?" WAS REALLY THE ONLY THING I COULD manage when, at my first ultrasound during my first pregnancy, the nurse told me there were *two babies*. How in the world was this possible? I'm a planner, type-A, must-have-everything-under-control kinda girl, and this news was unacceptable. I was more than ready to have one, adorable, preferably female, baby. Not two. No way, no how. Yet, here I was staring at a monitor that very clearly showed two little black dots.

Over time, as one would suspect, those little black dots grew, and they grew at an alarming rate. My husband and I could barely wrap our heads around the fact that we would be first-time parents of twins by the time they were born. There was a lot of drinking (by him) and swearing (by me) in the thirty-eight weeks before delivery. What was lacking was any real scientific basis regarding their twin-ness or whether they were identical or fraternal.

After hyperventilating the news to my family, I was reminded that my grandmother's sister on my mom's side had fraternal twin boys. *Did you follow that?* I was also researching like a madwoman, desperate for answers on just how the heck I was going to carry, deliver, and raise twins. A lot of what I read suggested that fraternal twins were hereditary on your maternal side and often skip a generation. I spoon-fed this information to the doctors and nurses who treated me, and they seemed to agree that the baby boys I was carrying were most likely fraternal. The ultrasounds also showed them each in a separate sac, further evidence of fraternal twins. We left it at that.

From the moment they were born, almost no one could tell them apart. Everywhere I took them (which wasn't many places because, really, who goes anywhere with two newborns?), people would just assume they were twins as in, "Oh, they're twins!" and the very next thing out of their mouths would be, "Oh, and they're identical!"

I would always respond, "They're actually fraternal." And then they would back away, slowly, from the crazy lady.

One day at the park, what can only be described as a pack of Latina women and their children were admiring the boys from afar. I started chatting with them about the twins, saying, "Yes, it's hard work, and, "Oh yes, they are double trouble."

Then came, "Oh, and they're identical."

I replied, "No, they're fraternal."

Silence. And then, "What about them is not identical?" They asked this in the same way Dirty Harry asked if you were, "Feeling lucky punk?"

So of course I agreed with them, like I had a moment of temporary insanity, and they started "God blessing" them again. Whew.

This went on for years. *Years.* This was not the kind of thing I thought I needed to be worried about when I first saw those ultrasound pictures. Who knew one of the hardest parts of having twins would be if I knew for certain if they were fraternal or identical? So I started looking around at other sets of multiples.

I have a best friend who has fraternal twin girls. The girls look almost nothing alike, and no one has ever had trouble telling them apart. In fact, no fraternal twins I've ever met have looked as alike as my boys do. Their own relatives cannot tell them apart!

Early on, whenever this topic came up, my husband was adamant of them being fraternal twins. He thinks because *he* can tell them apart easily, that proves they are fraternal. When I started to get skeptical, he immediately shut it down, and so began the feud.

Where they or weren't they? How the hell could I not know if my own kids were fraternal or identical? Colossal mom fail. Of course, dad thought he was winning.

The fallout from this epic debate is that we look like morons at parties, when we introduce our kids anywhere, or basically anytime the topic of the twins comes up, which is always! I introduce the boys now as identical, and I get the "look" from my husband that says, "We don't know for sure if they're identical, and I don't believe they are," to which I look back at him with something that says, "You're insane, and please don't make me explain your insanity to strangers." It's a shit-show.

Now, mind you, my husband calls the boys by the wrong name. A lot. Especially when we're in crowded places like theme parks or not crowded places, like our own home. And, to look at them from behind, it's impossible to tell them apart! It's most often we mix them up when they're running away from us (sometimes into traffic), and we do the stutter name call, "Mi, um, Vaug, Mi ..." and then have to look at the *other* one to see who may be heading toward disaster, before we call out the correct name. It's downright hazardous and still my husband doesn't believe.

One such incident left one of the boys yelling back at my husband, "Dad, I'm Miles!" because he was yelling at Vaughn to stop doing something. Of course, Vaughn continued right on doing what he was doing since my husband was screaming, "Miles! Stop doing that now!" when Miles was standing next to him, doing nothing, except perhaps wondering how his own father doesn't know who he is. Therapy is imminent.

This perfect storm brewed to a frothy head one evening, after the boys were in bed. I told my husband there was only really one true way to find out if the boys were identical or fraternal, and that was though a rather expensive blood test. In my mother's mind, it was of the utmost importance to know this detail about your kids in case of an emergency. What type of emergency may require this level of detailed information I do not know, but still.

My husband, who is the opposite of frugal, balked at this suggestion and once again foolishly clung to his belief that he knew the boys were fraternal, and we would not be spending money on a blood test for something he already knows the answer to.

Oh really?

Commence eruption.

My memory of it now is worn, but I know my flurry of words involved "moron," "pigheaded," "ridiculous," and "insane"—in rapid-fire succession and repetition, with phrases sprinkled in like, "I need to know what my own twins are," "How can you be so stubborn," and, yes, I pulled the "I carried them for thirty-eight long weeks while you did nothing" card.

His chosen fighting words were "crazy town" (my place of permanent residence), "ridiculous," "absurd," and "no," with phases like, "I already know the boys are fraternal," "It's everyone else's problem if they can't tell them apart," and yes, he pulled the "I make the money in this house" card. Oh, no you didn't!

After that, I think I flashed the "I'm super hurt you would go there" look and went to bed.

You know how people love to give you the advice of "never go to bed angry"? Well, I think those people never sleep! I'm here to tell you that it's perfectly okay to go to bed angry.

The next morning, it was like it never happened. To my husband, it was something so off his radar that he shrugged off the whole thing and basically told me to just do whatever I wanted.

So, like most women, when given permission to actually do the thing I fought so hard for, I no longer wanted to do it.

Instead, back to the researching board I went and found out that identical twins can be in separate sacs in-utero, but if there is only one placenta and they look exactly alike, then there's a 95 percent chance they're identical twins!

I immediately called my doctor to get my delivery report (free of charge) and guess what? One placenta.

I skipped into the kitchen to give my husband the news and to gloat about being right once again, but to this very day, he still refuses to believe they are identical. Perhaps I should start researching what's wrong with him.

And that's how, after four years, I found out what everyone else already knew: I have identical twins. *Now who can convince my husband?*

ALLIE BURDICK IS A SWEAT ADDICT WHO GETS HER FIX RUNNING for Team Oiselle, cycling, and chasing after her five-year-old twin boys. On any given day, you can find her racing, freelance writing, reading, dreaming about yoga, and coming to terms with being a stay-at-home mom. Allie's blog, VITA - Train for Life, is all about hard work and motivation with a healthy kick of snark and hilarity. Allie currently teaches two weekly fitness classes near her home in the northeast where she and her husband like to live it up big!

Chicken Drums Divorce Planning

By Michelle Grewe

M Y HUSBAND AND I DON'T REALLY ARGUE. EVERY single argument about something important that we ever had goes something like this: I tell him what's up, he fake apologizes, and then he proceeds to resent me for being right. It truly gets under my skin, too, because I swear I can read his mind now on account of the fact that we have been married for almost ten years, and I get more mad at the things he's thinking than what he says. Then he starts getting angry at the things he thinks I'm thinking about what he's thinking. Basically, we have telepathic arguments, and they're heated, raw, and uncut.

I'm the aggressive one in our relationship. When it comes to communicating, I'm the proactive one. I don't really complain about him unless I find a humorous way to do so and then generalize it to all men on my blog somewhere as a way to vent it out. Sometimes, I confide in my mother or best friend, but that's usually just for the reassurance. Mostly, I'm the type to just tell him what is bothering me as it occurs. I take a no-bullshit approach where I seek instant closure. I don't like letting an issue haunt us for days or months at a time, even though they usually do. I'm fair about it. I justify his actions better than he could. I'll be the first to make excuses for him. I'm constantly trying to see things from his perspective, but I want to fix the problem, whatever it is. If it's my attitude, I will work hard to adjust it, but if it's something he's doing, I try every psychological route to resolving the issue.

One of the biggest bollockings my husband ever reaped was the day he said, early in our marriage, "You've gained weight. Other guys would have a problem with that, but I don't. I still love you."

I was like, "Really? Don't you dare come at me with passive-aggressive controlling shit like that ever again. Do you really think men wouldn't be interested in me because I gained weight? As if you're the only person who will love me even when I'm fat?" I know he was being sincere, and really trying to give a real compliment because he really just has no game, but I've seen guys do this to my friends. It starts out with back-handed compliments like that, geared to make a woman feel like he is the only man to be interested in her, and then it ends in an overly controlling environment. I'm not saying my husband was trying to be a sociopath, nor that it would end up that way, but people only do to you what you allow them to do to you. This was a boundary that was important to me.

Men may think I'm a bitch, but I won't be their bitch. And I do look like a bitch to my husband's friends, and even worse, his family in Puerto Rico who are stuck in 1950s gender roles. But the fact of the matter is, if I don't stand up for myself, who will?

Early in our marriage, we were both content with each other's flaws. It really was a world where we could be who we are without judgment from each other, no matter how ridiculous the flaw or how damaging it could be. I remember my husband telling me when we were dating, "Marriage will change a woman. It always does. She goes from being really nice and complacent to being a controlling bitch."

I always responded, "Marriage won't change me. Becoming a mother will." I was right on the money. Having kids did change me. No longer were some of his flaws (as well as many of mine) something I could live with.

But before that really sunk in, I remember the biggest argument we had was when our first baby was a few months old. We were living in Wyoming on a military base far away from friends, family, and any perceived or potential support, so it was just the two of us raising this kid on our own, having no possible clue as to what we were doing. And our baby cried a lot. She was like a colicky baby, except she didn't really grow out of it.

One day she was crying, as usual. I did everything I could think to do. I fed her. I burped her. We did the gas dance.

I was so ready for a break, and my husband was actually trying to help for once. This reminds me of the two times he did the dishes and broke the garbage disposal, twice. It's like his help isn't exactly what I call help.

I said, "Put her in her bouncy."

He retorted, "No she likes the swing."

I rebutted, "No, the bouncy is her favorite."

He returned, "No, the swing."

We actually ended up arguing for a good hour, with a baby crying in the foreground for most of it, about whether or not the baby preferred the bouncer or swing. In the end, we were both right. She loved both of them. We were also both wrong. Neither device got her to stop crying at that moment. She ended up soothing herself with tummy time.

As our marriage progressed, our arguments became more heated, resentful arguments. In fact, our arguments switched from a simple disagreement to one of us being really in the right and the other being stubbornly wrong. Our marriage has survived profiles on sex sites, sharing of nudey pics, lies, spending money behind backs, hitting on the opposite sex, Jerry Springer family drama, an insanity diagnosis, and a few other show-stopping, divorce-causing things. Despite all that we've been through, I have found the only person I can count on when the world is against me is him, and he, me. He is by far my best friend, and I am his.

Before I get into this story, I first want to point out I'm usually carefree and insanely lenient about things. One time I caught the husband messaging a woman from his hometown in Puerto Rico. It was in Spanish, so I had to get a translator, but I discovered he proposed to her, several times, and they frequently fantasized about each other to each other. To digress for a second, watching my husband hit on other women, I have confirmed that he really has no game. I really should start hitting on these women for him under his profile. And my reaction? Outside of tossing tips his way on Serenading 101, I asked him if he wanted us to fly her up here. Let her move in. I get to keep the master bedroom. Really, if she wants to marry him, she should be closer to his dirty laundry she should be cleaning instead of me. I'm serious. I searched plane tickets asking him what dates would be good for them. I was already re-decorating the room I was going to stick them in, and penciling in a life I could potentially have with a live-in babysitter.

Honestly, I just want him to be happy, and if another woman makes him happy, then so be it. He had a change of heart after I confronted him about the chat I found by accident. What really changed our mind? During one of the discussions about it in the car, the radio played Pink's "Just Give Me a Reason." Yes. Pink saved my marriage. She is one amazing woman and recipient of my Bad Ass of the Year award. Did you know she was bitten by Chuck Norris once? It's not true, but after three days of pain and agony, Chuck Norris cried. Yeah. That's the level she is on.

But of all the things that could have caused divorce, the one thing that got me saving money for the occasion was a huge argument because he did something worse than cheating. We were living in the country, and his sister was living with us for a few months. I had no idea at the time that she hated me with the passion of a thousand STDs. Her English wasn't that good yet, and my Spanish definitely sucks, so we rarely communicated. My husband was working a lot of twelve-hour shifts, as we needed the overtime, and while we were living in an area where I got the most help I ever received with my children from neighbors, and sometimes his sister would watch the kids so I could go grocery shopping, I was still busy. All the help didn't make me relax. All it did was make me up my game to have a cleaner house more often and to cook more meals. The kids weren't sleeping all night yet, so I was up around the clock where my only real sleep was an occasional nap at the mercy of my husband.

He would invariably wake me up two hours into it with, "I'm hungry. What's for dinner?"

I was like "Really? How about a plate of go-make-it-yourself?"

One delightful New Year's Eve, my husband and his sister decided to make dinner while I was napping. I would almost swear they were planning to outdo my cooking with their Puerto Rican cuisine they so much missed from their mother. When I woke up, my kitchen was destroyed. Mind you, we rented from an evil twat waffle who came by once a month and actually moved the refrigerator to make sure I had been cleaning under the fridge. She checked inside the oven, under the lamp-fan over the stove—everywhere had to be spotless beyond a military inspection because she feared cockroaches would otherwise move in.

So when I saw every pot and pan I owned dirty on the stove, every huge bowl full of grimy, slimy stuff, and green goo oozing from my blender and dripping all over my walls, the inside of the lamp above the stove, on the outside and inside of the cabinets, on the floor, and all over the counter tops, I was livid. It looked like Slimer from *The Ghostbusters* had jacked off all over my kitchen. The green stuff, by the way, was their attempt at *sofrito*, which isn't even the food itself. It's just an ingredient in the food, one they didn't use because they couldn't make it right.

But I got over the mess pretty quick since I was basking in the afterglow of the first good, four-hour nap ever in the time-space continuum, and at that point, I didn't have to cook dinner. I was kind of excited.

My husband then said, "Go ahead and get something to eat." A bowl of pasta salad with lunchmeat and one chicken drumstick hid among the mess like Waldo.

My child gave me puppy dog begging eyes, "Can I have that chicken, Mommy?"

Of course, I replied, "Yeah, sure love."

I looked in the freezer. There were still six frozen drumsticks. Yes, my husband and his sister, both of whom had earned a decent GPA through school, figured six drumsticks were more than enough to feed three adults and two children.

I grabbed a couple bites of the pasta salad, assuming it would taste awful, and it was, to my surprise, delicious. Listening to my husband and sister laugh profusely about things they were saying to each other in Spanish, I frequently asked, "What's so funny?" and nobody would translate. They literally ignored me like I wasn't in the room, and between that, the messy kitchen, and the frozen, uncooked drumsticks, my attitude was getting uncontrollably darker.

I went to snatch some seconds from the huge bowl full of pasta salad since I had only given myself enough to preview it. While they made enough drumsticks to feed only my husband, they made enough pasta salad to feed a football team after practice. I grabbed the spoon, scooped out a scoop, plopped it on my plate, and grabbed a second spoonful. The husband interrupts (now I exist), "Whoa whoa whoa! What are you doing?"

Confused, I responded, "Getting seconds."

He blurted, obviously without any thought before or after, "I need all this for work tomorrow."

I put the food back and walked out the door. I decided, "Screw them. I'll go get my own dinner somewhere." I was so livid that he denied me food after all those years I cooked for him, I was shaking. This was way worse than the time he ate all the Reese's Peanut Butter Cups, my top craving, which I had stashed in the freezer when I was pregnant. We lived in the country, so I had approximately three fast food options, all of which were closed for New Year's.

I called my friend in town, in tears (yes, in tears over dinner) proclaiming that I was, at that point, a single lady. I threw my rings in the ashtray. She lived a half-hour drive away, and I joined her at the club, dressed like a frumpy housewife, getting there about five minutes after the countdown to a new year. Between the empty stomach and the adrenaline from the empty stomach, I was so drunk that I had to crash at my friend's house. I didn't get home until probably 8:00 a.m. I wanted to cheat on my husband just to make him as angry as I was, but I was not drunk enough to touch any of the options, like the beer goggles were broken that night, so I just insinuated that I cheated on him when I got home. He probably still to this day thinks I slept with someone that night. I still don't care. I was single that night. If he liked it then he should have put a ring on it and made it dinner it was permitted to eat.

At that point, I decided it was time to make some long-term goals. Yes, denying me food is worse than cheating on me. Anyhow, I needed a career again, some money in savings, a job, a place to live, and childcare. I had my work cut out for me. I started saving money. Five months later, my husband was laid off. My savings then contributed to living expenses, and by then, I was kind of over the dinner thing. Our relationship really improved when his sister moved back home.

I did clean the kitchen myself. My husband is now allowed to cook with the grill. We are finally getting to a point where he can occasionally make pancakes, but he will never be allowed to make *sofrito* again. Oh, and I get first dibs on the big piece of meat—which I usually give to him.

Michelle Grewe is a mom, veteran, monster hit man, bouncer, twenty questions master, semi-professional diamond thief, mad scientist, human jungle gym, and a terrible driver. She paints, blogs at Crumpets and Bollocks, plays piano badly, and dabbles in T-shirt design and fontography. She also doesn't fold underwear, and she eats loads of gluten.

The Wedding Shower Heist

By Barb Godshalk

IT HAPPENED AROUND TWELVE YEARS AGO WITH MY then-fiancé John. It was supposed to be a simple forty-five minute trip to my mother's house. I was told we were going there to help my parents clean their huge, inground pool. In retrospect, I should have seen it coming. John fit into my family as if he'd always been there. The very fact that I was even engaged at all was still a shock.

This little soap opera began about a year before. I met a nice small business owner named Dan at a singles-group function. Dan was cute, intelligent, and very much into the outdoors. (A perfect match for a city-born bug wussy like me!) My idea of roughing it is no cable. I'm still working on my problem.

Needless to say, things didn't work out between us. Before he ran off into the hills screaming, Dan introduced me to his friend, John. He was convinced we'd be perfect for each other. (My perspective? Terrific. I've got the hots for you, but you want me date your friend!)

Reluctantly, I agreed to talk to John on the phone, and it felt like I had known him a very long time. The first time I saw him, I mentally prepared that let's-just-be-friends speech I had heard as much as I had given. And then it came—the moose trap! At the end of our first date, John handed me a Beanie Baby moose. It's still my copilot in the car.

What's the big, fat, hairy deal about a moose? It was a sign! Moose just so happened to be a nickname I stuck my poor father with when I was a kid. It started out as more of a fat joke. (My diplomatic skills developed early.) Over the years, it became an affectionate nickname he tolerated from me, but it was not something he went by.

John knew all about this from the conversations we had leading up to our first date. Hence the dilemma—a man who listened to me! Holy crap, he was paying attention! What do I do now? I can't not go out with him again; I'd be a total jerk. Oh well, maybe this will end up being another person I can just do stuff with. And so we did. We went to movies, dinners, and even a murder mystery with some friends. He was finishing my sentences in a way that, under other circumstances, would have creeped me out.

After about nine months of dating, John started kicking around the idea of ring shopping. I wasn't quite sure he was serious. After all, I was pretty much on the fence about the whole thing and wondering if I should be dating someone I didn't really feel physically attracted to. I remember talking about this with my best friend, at the time.

She told me something like, "You know, they don't come with neon signs pointing at them saying, 'This is the one.'"

"But I need that!" I said.

It turns out that John was deadly serious, and once I realized he was my best friend, getting engaged was a no-brainer. How ironic that I had recently spent seven years with a commitment-phobic person, yet I ended up with someone who proposed within a year! Even more strange was that he was actively participating in wedding planning. I think he assumed an active role as I was still unsure and focused on moving out of my apartment. He took care of a lot of the nuptial legwork.

We had been taking so many car trips for errands during those months, what was one more? I don't remember the actual reason we had a fight in the car. I'm not even sure which car it was, mine or his. I can tell you it was probably exacerbated by two things. We were late, as usual, and had to drive in New Jersey. Punctuality has never been in my repertoire, and many of my friends would say it could snow in July before I ever get my act together. I am grateful we at least knew where we were going as getting lost with your significant other can be as stressful on your relationship as clothes shopping.

I believe at the time I'd been sucked into my own little personal vortex without taking a moment to step back to see the bigger picture. I missed a few details like: it was only a month or two before our wedding, we never helped my parents clean the pool before, why were we going there on a Sunday afternoon, and so on.

While I am one of those people who would have been late for her own wedding without continuous prodding, my feathers were still ruffled from John hassling me out the door. We got in the car and started off toward my mom's house. I have no clear recollection of who said what exactly, but it may have started with a comment about my driving skills and gone downhill from there. (Guys, commenting on your mate's driving is a lot like waking a sleeping giant regardless of the truth.)

As the argument progressed, I was beginning to worry about what this fight meant. *Is he getting too angry? Was this a bad sign for our relationship? Was I making a huge mistake? What's with the ear hair?* I'd like to be able to say this was just pre-wedding jitters. But, no, I pretty much analyze the bejeezus out of everything.

By the time we got out of the car in my mother's driveway, we were arguing loudly and waving our arms like a couple of mobsters. Mom was nervously looking out the front door wondering what was going on and worried I was going to call off the wedding. I had been engaged once before. I looked over and recognized my uncle's car. Then I noticed my sister's. Then I realized the driveway was filled with familiar cars. Finally, it occurred to me: this was my wedding shower. I was dressed in a ratty T-shirt and shorts, looking, in my estimation, one step above home-less. I looked at John and quietly said, "You bastard." He just grinned. We are approaching our twelfth anniversary.

BARB GODSHALK IS THE PROUD MOMMY OF A NOW FIVE-YEAR-OLD daughter and lives in South Jersey with her amazing husband. Her work has been featured on the radio, online at In the Powder Room, and the Writers' Group anthology, *Tall Tales and Short Stories from South Jersey*. She writes largely memoir pieces relating life lessons as she lives with a walking wealth of material. Barb has been a member of the South Jersey Writers' Group since 2007.

Fetus, Take the Wheel

By Amanda Mushro

S OME WOMEN CREATE ELABORATE BIRTH PLANS THAT consist of lights dimmed in the labor room, soft music playing in the background, a few bounces on a birthing ball, a doula on hand, and maybe a water birth with dolphins. But my birthing plan was pretty simple: a doctor will give me an epidural, and then a doctor will hand me a healthy baby.

Because women like to tell horrifying stories to soon-to-be mothers, I had heard dozens of cautionary tales of women not making it to the hospital in time and their doctors looking at them grim-faced, quietly whispering, "I'm sorry, but it's too late for an epidural." That's usually where the stories would stop because any further details were just too cruel to elaborate upon when a pregnant lady was present.

I've watched a lot of *Grey's Anatomy*, so I'm pretty much an expert on the whole birthing process, and the only way to ensure you don't give birth in the hospital parking lot without an epidural is making sure your husband gets you to the hospital in time for that procedure. I would do all the heavy lifting and pushing of pregnancy and labor, but I gave the man that put my bun in the oven, my husband, the extremely important job of ensuring we get to the hospital in a timely manner.

I had nothing to worry about because I knew my man was taking his job seriously. Much like my ideas on parenting pre-kids, oh how wrong I was.

My labor started on the eve before my due date. What began as, "Ouch, I think I just had a contraction," escalated to, "Sweet Jesus, get me some drugs!" in less than an hour.

With my hospital bag already packed, my husband, Aaron, helped me waddle to the car, and looking over my shoulder, I asked, "You know where we are going, right?"

"Babe, c'mon. Of course I do."

Since my birth plan consisted of drugs and a baby, I decided to forgo the whole hospital tour. Honestly, I was happy being blissfully unaware of what was really going to go down once I was admitted, but I knew the man I married a million moons ago would get precise directions to the hospital that was forty-five minutes away from our home.

Wincing through another powerful contraction, the car began to swerve across a few lanes before Aaron sharply turned the wheel to get it straight.

"What are you doing?" I asked.

"Nothing, nothing. Keep breathing," he replied.

"You keep breathing, and keep your eyes on the road," I growled.

He couldn't keep his eyes on the road because his eyes were on his phone. I noticed what was on the screen, MapQuest. He was searching for directions.

"Why are you looking up directions now? I thought you knew where you were going?"

"I just want to double-check."

"You have no idea where we're going. Do you?"

"No, I have an idea."

The only thing that saved him in that moment was the contraction raging across my back and down my legs. Wincing in pain, I threatened to get out of the car and hoof it solo to the hospital or just push that baby right out there in the car.

He took the very next exit off the highway, and I assumed he had the hospital in his sights. Oh, what a relief, I don't need to be a widow before my child is born.

I peeked up from the fetal position long enough to see out the window that this was not the hospital. In fact, it wasn't really a *nice* neighborhood. "Sketchy" came to mind. This was the type of neighborhood you only end up in when you make a wrong turn. The kind of neighborhood where you lock your doors and don't ask for directions.

"I cannot believe I'm in labor and you are driving me through an episode of *COPS*!"

"Babe, just calm down. I'll find the hospital. Just let me pull over and MapQuest it."

"Oh my god! Do not pull over, or we will surely die in this car! Just drive!"

After a few turns and quick driving past a few questionable characters on street corners, we were back on track or so he assured me.

From the highway, I could see the hospital off in the distance. It was like a mirage, and I was a stranded traveler in the desert looking for water, or in my case, a big needle in my back.

"There it is! There it is! How do we get to it? You get me to that hospital, or I will never make another baby with you again."

"Calm down, crazy pregnant lady."

"You did this to me!"

"You asked me to!"

That's when we both saw it: a sign for the hospital's emergency room. He stepped on the gas and screeched into the parking lot like he was on *Dukes of Hazzard*. The car was barely at a standstill when I threw open the door and made a beeline for the ER doors. Aaron ran up behind me with my bag and tried to help me by holding onto my arm, but I gave him a quick jab to his kidneys.

Before being wheeled down a long hall to labor and delivery, I grabbed Aaron by the shirt collar and whispered in his ear, "If I missed my epidural window, you'd better find a YouTube video that tells you how to give one. Got it?" Once I was all set up in a labor and delivery suite and assured by the nurses the epidural could happen if we moved fast, I allowed Aaron to come in with the understanding he was on probation and was only allowed inside for the good of our unborn child.

I passed the time waiting for the anesthesiologist to arrive by grinding my teeth and clawing my nails down the side of the hospital bed during each contraction. Through sweat and tears, I could see Aaron staring at his phone for a minute or two then looking up at me with wide eyes.

Ugh, another contraction. *Dammit, why didn't I go to a birthing class and learn all about the hee-hee-haw-haw breathing? Too late now.*

Contraction over, and he's looking at his phone again. A minute later, he looks up, and another contraction starts. Through excruciating back labor, I scream, "What the hell are you doing?"

"I'm timing your contractions," he answered, resetting the timer on his phone.

"I don't need you to time them now. We're already at the hospital. Just get out there and find out where the hell my epidural is!"

With the speed of a gazelle, he bounded out the door and retuned moments later with a man surrounded in light who floated on air. His melodic voice rang out as he said these sweet words to me, "Hello, I'm here to give you your epidural."

"She's really been looking forward to seeing you," laughed my husband, but that silly grin was quickly wiped off his face when I barked some incomprehensible response at him.

I welcomed that giant needle in my back and its sweet relief. Like a magic spell had been cast, I didn't feel a single thing below the belt, and the need to punch my husband in the balls during each contraction melted away.

An hour later, my beautiful boy came into the world, and maybe it was the drugs or maybe it was just pure happiness, but when I laid eyes on my baby, I knew he needed to be named after his father. Even though I was planning how I was going to exact my revenge, he is still the best man I've ever known, and I love and adore that fool. After all, I'm a pill to live with. I'm bossy, demanding, overly emotional, and a lousy housekeeper. On top of that, I don't reciprocate back rubs, and I often say things like, "I'll cut you if you don't stop snoring." And through all of that, Aaron still loves me.

Marriage is all about compromise, and after this incident, I compromised by not plotting his demise in his sleep, and he promised to always know where the hospital is and to rub my feet for the rest of our lives.

AMANDA MUSHRO IS THE WRITER BEHIND THE HILARIOUS MOMMY blog, Questionable Choices in Parenting. Sometimes she thinks she is doing a great job as a mom, but then she does something that makes her question her own parenting abilities. She lives in Maryland with her husband and kids and tries every day to laugh at life as a parent so they don't commit her. Her writing has been featured on Scary Mommy, In the Power Room, and The Huffington Post. She was a cast member of Listen to Your Mother: Washington DC and has essays featured in the four anthologies.

How to Talk to a Man—
Are You Listening to
Me?

By Chris Carter

COMMUNICATING WITH OUR SPOUSES IS SOMETHING OF an art in which we display the unique dialogue that can either be a sure success or a magnificent mess. I've had the excruciating honor of navigating this tiring terrain for fifteen years with my husband, and I will share with you the valuable insights I have painfully gained along the way.

There are a few concepts that are crucial to understanding the inner workings of a man and how they interpret our words. More importantly, there are steps we must all take in order for our guys to actually hear our words in the first place. Although I continue to be amazed at the limitations that we must carefully overcome, there is hope that you, too, can discover and put into practice the ability to be heard.

How amazing would that be?

I know. It seems so—unattainable.

But fear not! All it takes is the three C's of Communication! *Constant. Conscious. Compromising.* Yep! That's it! In order to adhere to the three C's, I have outlined a step-by-step program that will teach you how to navigate through the faults of our men.*

Behind every man is a one-step plan.

I've learned that if I give my husband more than one instruction at the same time, he will not be able to process any of the aforementioned instructions. Our guys can only handle one concept, one task, one thought at a time. For example, when I'm leaving the house and he needs to cover dinner for the kids:

There is pasta in the fridge with a container of sauce to heat up and pour over it. I also have green beans for you to steam.

I lost him at pasta. Seriously. He's gone. His face contorts into that confused, squinting stare, whereby his natural instinct is to turn the switch off. Oftentimes, the silence will be your cue if you can't see his face. Sometimes he will then question where the pasta is, because that is all he heard and could not process anything more that came from your mouth.

If he asks you a question? The poor man is trying! Give him a smile. Gently guide him to the fridge and remove said dinner contents. Point to each item as you speak slowly, while simplifying your words to two syllables:

Pasta.

Sauce over.

Beans, steam.

You see what I did there? This works 90 percent of the time. However, there are those difficult days where nothing sinks in. You will be cued in to this if the silence is combined with him walking away while distracting himself with another task. At this point, you must simply surrender your plan and hang onto hope that the kids will be fed something that night.

Do not, I repeat, do not get angry. Just walk away and wish him a lovely evening. This is key, for there should be no arguments over something as simple as a meal.

Remember ladies, this "one-step" man needs our help with grocery lists too. Do not tell him to pick up more than one item at the store without giving him a list! Even if you truly believe he will master two items in his mind, be assured he will only come back with one of those items, or you may simply get a text or a phone call innocently inquiring about the second item. He can only handle ONE thing. ONE thing.

Onward—

If you need something done that you cannot do, you must ask this of him two weeks before said thing needs to be done.

By Chris Carter

Our men are busy! They have a lot on their plates and even more on their minds. Although we might feel as though our request should be addressed immediately, we must selflessly wait with utter patience. The task in question may be more important to you than to him. And honestly? His forgetfulness and fleeting thoughts are born from his concrete concepts that dwell in the here and now. Once you ask something of him, within seconds, he will not remember what you asked. Therefore, you need to remind him each day for two weeks straight. Use a gentle tone with a prefix of, "I know you're busy but," or even write a cute honey-do note for him. Do not, I repeat, do not ask for more than one thing at a time!

In this case, I am merely talking about those wishes that are not life threatening or critical to your family's safety. Those requests must turn swiftly into ongoing requests that very day, hour, and even minute—depending on the severity of the circumstance. These tasks are usually accomplished successfully, because our men are great at responding to a crisis in order to protect the ones they love.

If you really need your husband to listen, you must turn off all technical devices, be in close proximity to him, shut off all surrounding sound, and tell him this is important.

Our men are easily distracted. They also don't discriminate between serious conversations and functional interactions. They need silence and stillness in order to tune into our words and truly listen to our hearts when we share them. It can happen if the atmosphere is created for cultivation. Our men love us, and they want to be present in our lives and in our hearts. We simply must accept that the path to getting there can be filled with mishaps. Our guys need help with their intentions. The key here is to get his undivided attention, which can be quite challenging with our men.

Do not be misled by two moves men often make: 1) eye contact, and 2) muttering "okay."

If your man makes eye contact while you are speaking to him, this is deceiving! Do not fall for the illusion of listening. Just because your man is looking you straight in the eye does not imply that he is mentally processing your words. When your well-intentioned man says "okay" in response to what you say, do not believe that he has taken note of it and will remember. This is an instinctive and conditioned response that is empty of meaning.

You see, oftentimes we tell our guys what will be going on in the short term and long term, and we assume they have heard the plan and will execute said plan when they look at us and say, "okay."

This isn't the case at all. If you believe this to be true, then you will surely snap when he asks what the plan is a mere five minutes later. You will positively pop when he texts you five hours later asking who is picking your kid up from soccer. And you will certainly scream when he doesn't make the calls or set the reservations in advance for said plan.

By all means, you must never trust these two misleading moves if you want your plans executed properly.

Now it's time to apply these newly learned tips and tricks when communicating with your man. Don't forget, it's all about *Constant. Conscious. Compromising.* Apply these steps in talking with your man and surely you won't wonder, "Are you listening to me?" It's tough terrain out there, but I have every hope that you will learn the fine art of communicating with your man and rest assured—you WILL be heard!

Good luck, ladies. You're gonna need it.

*This program is not approved by the National Board of Married Men, but personal data shows positive results.

CHRIS CARTER IS A STAY-AT-HOME MOM OF TWO PRETTY AMAZING kids. When she's not running her kids around town to various sporting events or hosting her women's group and leading her Church Youth Ministry, you will find her at her laptop writing her heart out—sharing deep thoughts and significant moments. She has been writing at TheMomCafe.com for almost four years, where she hopes to encourage mothers everywhere through her humor, inspiration, and faith. She has been a regular contributor to 1Corinthians13 Parenting, Mothering from Scratch, and SheShares Ministries. She has also published her own book, *Maddening and Marvelous Motherhood*, in addition to having the honor of contributing to both *The Mother of all Meltdowns* and *Marriage Hacks*.

How to Talk to a Woman—Without Sacrificing Your Cajones

By Eli Pacheco

EVER WONDER HOW THE FIRST PILGRIMS AND AMERICAN Indians reached a point at which they could communicate with one another? One had to be heard *and* understood—preferably without eating a musket or an arrow. Someone had to step up and man up to get the ball rolling.

It still happens today. You see it when an argument between a Japanese midfielder and Puerto Rican goalkeeper is mitigated by a Romanian soccer referee. Miracles do happen. Sometimes even Democrats and Republicans carry on a conversation on Capitol Hill. And once in a while, a dude will communicate with a woman. He'll talk. He'll listen. Even, sometimes, when the wind is right and the pollen count is down, he'll comprehend.

We men fuel the stereotype that in the male half of the species, cognitive development stalled right around the time of Homo habilis (you know, the early man, circa 2.4 million to 1.4 million years ago, commonly known as the inventor of stone tools).

Trust me. I know what I'm talking about. I've always been outnumbered by the women in my life. My lapel is loaded with medals in a long and illustrious career in which I've been—at times, simultaneously—a dad, son, brother to a sister, husband, boyfriend, coach of girls' soccer teams (more than once of teenage and prepubescent girls), and, in junior high, I was a thespian who wore makeup, tights, and had a kissing scene. (I once played a prince, if you're wondering). I covered women's sports as a writer too.

And, at nearly forty-three years of age, I'm still standin'. *How's that for credentials?*

How to talk to women—this stuff is gold, boys. Like The Force, you must use it for good only. Like karate, it should be used primarily for self-defense. Don't gloat, don't flaunt, and don't misuse it. If women believe we've figured this out—there's a protocol for an instant sea change, and it took us seventy-three years to get where we are. Don't doom your sons and grandsons.

Here's how to talk to a woman—without sacrificing your cajones:

Show some capacity for cognitive thinking.

Admittedly, the bar is set lower than a centipede's jock itch. We fellas are considered simple mouth-breathers with ADHD so severe the sight of a rack of ribs or slightest side boob derails the most determined train of thought. Don't feed the propaganda, mates.

Women don't understand the complexity of our thoughts. Nor should they be expected to.

They don't understand how easily our thoughts can drift to memories of a little-league RBI double as they're telling us a shopping story. Or how having a shopping list dictated to us, with the slightest of pause, can result in us filling in the silence with words like bratwurst, beef jerky, and barbecue.

When they speak, stop moving. Get your hands off the keyboard. Put down the remote. Pull your hand out of the front of your pants. Listen like you're about to check in as a third-down back for the Ravens and coach John Harbaugh is giving you the next play. Pay attention.

Understand her game plan.

Just as you and I fight to shatter the misconceptions, she has a few of her own. She might not constantly analyze what we say and how we say it. She might not conspire with her girlfriends to conclude that we're worthless dolts who need to be more like Ryan Gosling in *The Notebook*.

She does think differently, though. When we put head to pillow at night, it's seconds before the snoring and dreams of Jennifer Lawrence and muscle cars commence. Meanwhile, every complexity of life forces opens your lady's eyelids. How ironic that women grow up with dolls whose eyes shut when laid down, yet they grow up and do the exact opposite.

The sloth that our brain becomes at bedtime contrasts the hamster on Red Bull that hers becomes. Understand this. Understand that she'll ask you if you turned off the grill or paid the Home Depot bill or ever wrote that thank-you card to the DJ from your wedding reception. Seventeen years ago.

A woman believes God created the world in six days, and if there was a woman around for the seventh that would be the day she had to correct everything from making mangoes easier to slice, to helping pandas actually defend themselves in the wild.

She'll say it's a man's world, but it desperately needs a woman's touch.

Just listen to her. What's most important to her will be easy to pick out. Depending on your lady, a raised eyebrow, higher pitched voice, or slight snarl of the lip will be all the indication you need.

Be a man.

Being a man means balance between Steven Seagal and Tom Hanks. It means listening is important, but without a backbone, you might as well be tofu at a tailgate party—never, ever taken seriously.

A man doesn't need to be Super Man; he just needs to be a man who is super. I've always absorbed harsh words from a coach, but from a woman or girl, I let them slice me. This is harmful. It keeps me from demonstrating the strength I need for her and for me, and it diminishes the faith a daughter or female boss or significant other can have in me.

A fragile psyche puts you in the same bucket as the wildebeest with a limp. You'll become lunch.

To man up is more than a slippery slope. It's a forty-five-degree drop covered in melted butter with lava-swimming piranhas waiting below you. To man up is equal parts resolve, patience, reassurance, confidence, wit, fast thinking, and slow talking, all with good posture and great-smelling aftershave.

To win in the game of gender communication isn't to get everything right. Perfection just sets us up for failure. Our flaws are our respites. Yes, we can build flower boxes and landscape like a Martinez. But we struggle to fold towels and load a dishwasher to the strict rule of a woman.

That's okay. Even if we've mastered the laundry-load balance and conquered bargain shopping, to display that prowess would only be showing off. And then it's expected of us.

We guys—we're just smart enough to know how dumb we are about some things.

And that extra time?

Well, it allowed Homo habilis to invent the first stone tools.

What will you do with it?

ELI PACHECO IS A COACH, WRITER, AND DAD. SOMETIMES, ALL AT once. Sometimes, it's hard to see the difference! That's why he blogs at Coach Daddy.

A Note From the Editor

Thank you for reading *Clash of the Couples*. We invite you to visit our individual blogs and connect with us on social media. Each writer in this book can be found on networks like Facebook, Goodreads, Twitter, Instagram, Pinterest, and more. You can find the links on the book's landing page at www.bluelobsterbookco.com/books/clashofthecouples. We sincerely hope that you enjoyed our crazy stories. If you did like the book, please share with all of your friends, family, co-workers, and the couple bickering next you at Applebee's. When you're done spreading the word, could you leave us a review on Amazon? It only takes a minute or two and really helps increase the visibility of the book. Thank you!

Time to find something else to read? If you loved *Clash of the Couples*, then you might enjoy Blue Lobster Book Co.'s original publication *The Mother of All Meltdowns*, which is available on Amazon and B&N.com. Every mother, at some point, inevitably becomes her own worst enemy. In a millisecond, her halo crumbles and she has a moment so crazed it is forever known as the one—the mother of all meltdowns. Some of today's hottest bloggers bare all (well, not quite like that) in this eye-opening, mind-blowing anthology. Be prepared to laugh, cry, and have your mouth fall open in disbelief. At times, they are so far from angelic, they make Attila the Hun look like Mother Teresa.

Thanks again for all of your support!

Crystal Ponti

CPSIA information can be obtained at www.ICGtesting.com
Printed in the USA
LVOW09s1114150215

427113LV00015B/528/P